Buying
and
Wearing
Classic
Vintage
Clothes

Vintage
STYLE

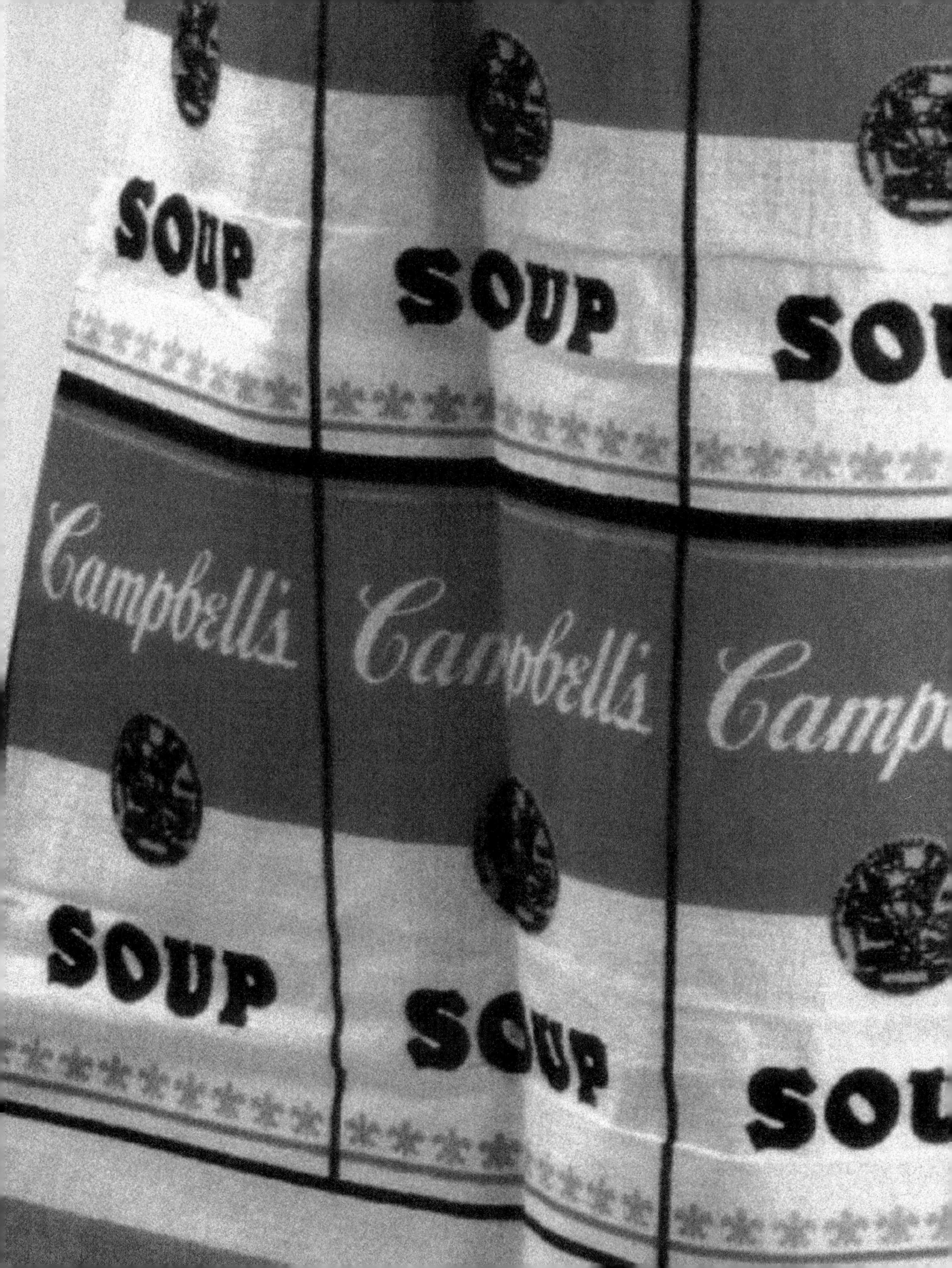
SOUP
SOUP
Campbell's
Campbell's
SOUP
SOUP
SOUP

Buying
and
Wearing
Classic
Vintage
Clothes

Vintage
STYLE

Tiffany Dubin   Ann E. Berman

With photographs by Hollister Lowe

HarperCollins*Publishers*

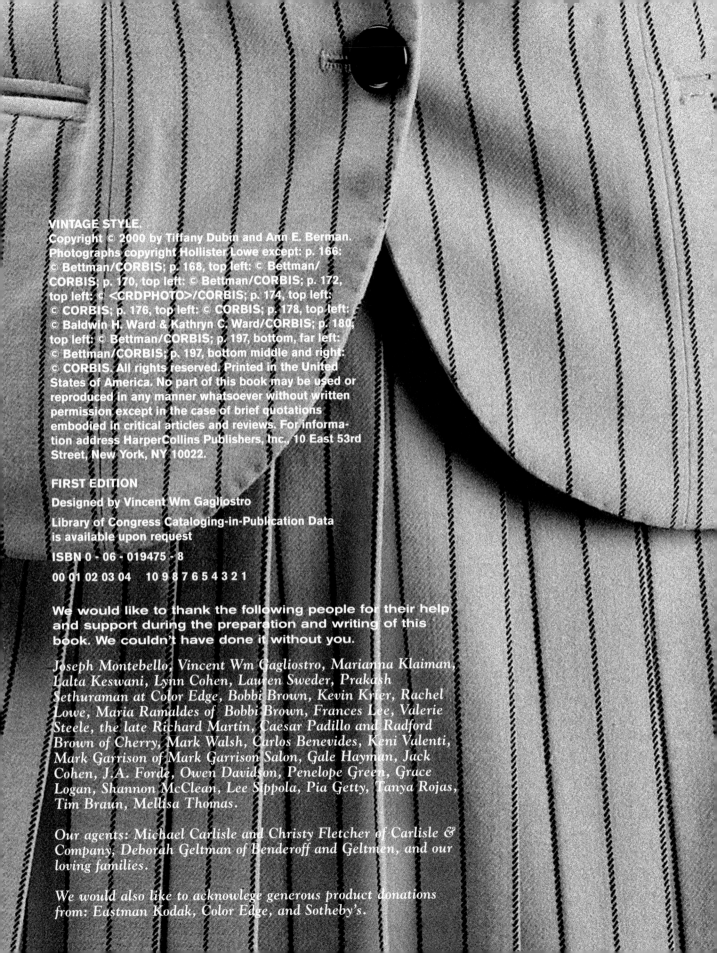

FIRST EDITION

Designed by Vincent Wm Gagliostro

Library of Congress Cataloging-in-Publication Data
is available upon request

ISBN 0 - 06 - 019475 - 8

00 01 02 03 04   10 9 8 7 6 5 4 3 2 1

We would like to thank the following people for their help
and support during the preparation and writing of this
book. We couldn't have done it without you.

Joseph Montebello, Vincent Wm Gagliostro, Marianna Klaiman,
Lalta Keswani, Lynn Cohen, Lauren Sweder, Prakash
Sethuraman at Color Edge, Bobbi Brown, Kevin Krier, Rachel
Lowe, Maria Ramaldes of Bobbi Brown, Frances Lee, Valerie
Steele, the late Richard Martin, Caesar Padillo and Radford
Brown of Cherry, Mark Walsh, Carlos Benevides, Keni Valenti,
Mark Garrison of Mark Garrison Salon, Gale Hayman, Jack
Cohen, J.A. Forde, Owen Davidson, Penelope Green, Grace
Logan, Shannon McClean, Lee Sippola, Pia Getty, Tanya Rojas,
Tim Braun, Mellisa Thomas.

Our agents: Michael Carlisle and Christy Fletcher of Carlisle &
Company, Deborah Geltman of Benderoff and Geltmen, and our
loving families.

We would also like to acknowlege generous product donations
from: Eastman Kodak, Color Edge, and Sotheby's.

the movie
actress
climbed
gracefully
out of the
limo...

KODAK TX 6043

Introduction
Why Vintage?

Her deep blue velvet gown, expertly cut on the bias, had an unusual richness and sheen and clung perfectly to her curves. It was the choice of a woman who could have anything she wanted and who knew how to make herself stand out—even in this jaded Oscar-night crowd. But when the dazzled interviewer asked, no designer could take credit. The dress had been made by an unknown French dressmaker in the late 1930s and purchased at a vintage clothing store for $280.

vintage

is hot

Vintage is readily available and it's just the boost your wardrobe needs to make it more versatile and individual. But where to begin? How do you find the right vintage clothes for your lifestyle and body type and incorporate them into your contemporary wardrobe? If you ever wondered about vintage—what all the fuss is about and what it can do for your fashion image—this is the book for you.

If you think you know vintage, think again. Once funky and low-budget—the province of starving design and drama students—the vintage world is going mainstream. Banish those images of boogie-woogie bugle boy platforms, limp Victorian chemises, and pink poodle skirts. The new market is all about classic cuts, timeless fabrics—the beautiful shapes and constructions that appear again and again throughout the 20th century. The quality and detailing of these noncouture, readily available vintage

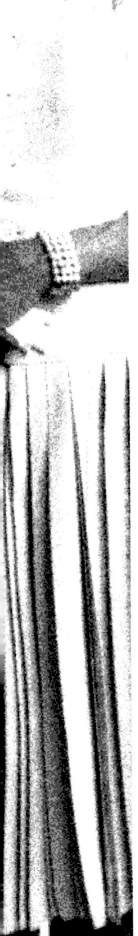

clothes will come as a startling revelation. Only the most expensive garments made today can touch them.

What exactly is "classic"? We're talking about the simple, timeless clothes that are as wearable today as the day they were made. They are pure of line and unfussy, never gimmicky or faddish. We're talking about perfectly cut '60s chemise dresses, sleek black '50s capri pants à la Audrey Hepburn, buttery soft leather jackets, hot Pucci prints—all easy to mix and match with contemporary pieces from your wardrobe. There are vintage blazers waiting out there by the dozens, finished with handmade buttons and striped silk linings, and black satin cocktail dresses that might have been made yesterday—all at a fraction of the price of their modern sisters. Vintage boutiques are springing up all over the country, auction houses have added specialty departments to handle the interest, and the Internet buzzes with bidders, all buying to wear. Vintage has become a legitimate alternative fashion choice.

Only two decades ago it was a very different story. The vintage world was still a tiny place inhabited by a handful of pioneering retailers and their arty clientele—often women active in the fine or performing arts who were anxious to set themselves apart from the common horde. The vintage buyer of yesterday tended to favor complete "outfits"—like a '40s patterned rayon dress, worn with platforms, a peplum jacket, and a snood. Victorian bridal gowns were also big sellers, along with '20s beaded dresses destined for upscale costume parties or, more daringly, to be flaunted in front of conservative relatives at family weddings. Such clothes were chosen precisely because they screamed their vintage origins—proclaiming the wearer to be above the whims of fashion, who wished to be admired for her individuality and daring.

Only a lonely few recognized the startling modernity of vintage classics and bought them simply to be beautifully dressed. In 1980, for example, bestselling author Judith Krantz created a Russian-American character, Princess Daisy, a classy but temporarily poverty-stricken heroine. We find Daisy rooting among her London jumble-shop finds, determined to find an outfit to disguise her distressed financial circumstances and impress the hostess of an upcoming country-house weekend: "Triumphantly she held up an ensemble from the late 1930s when the daring Schiaparelli was doing clothes which were four decades ahead of their time. There was a jacket in lettuce green tweed touched with sequins at the lapels, worn with a pair of corduroy pants in a darker shade of green. 'Just right, don't you think?' " Daisy crows, putting fake emeralds in her hair and sallying forth to wow the assembled company.

Daisy was lucky to get away with her charade because she dates from an era of fashion history—not so long ago—when anything not being "shown" in a particular season was considered "out of style." Designers were still calling the tune and women had to dance to it. If trousers were declared to be slim for a season, anything else would automatically look dated. Hemlines rose and fell according to the same dictates; shoulder pads came in and out. It was possible to characterize the "look" of a historical decade, declaring "miniskirts were '60s" and "pouf skirts were '80s" with complete authority.

But times have changed. According to Gale Hayman, beauty and style writer and founder of the legendary Giorgio's of L.A., we've been enjoying this new freedom since 1985. "About that time a flag went up," Hayman says. "Women decided they would no longer be dictated to by designers. Individuality became the most important thing—that and comfort—because the pace of life had quickened so much and we wanted to feel comfortable in our clothes." Penelope Green, a fashion columnist for *The New York Times*, points out another fashion milestone: "In about 1995 the entire 20th century of fashion suddenly became open to 'pillaging' by fashionable women," she explains. "Tom Ford [the Creative Director of Gucci] was a big part of that. Anything up to the '60s was already being worn, but he made it okay to add shapes from the '70s and '80s to the mix."

Designers have loosened the leash of fashion dogma, allowing women to choose their own individual look within an increasingly varied palette of styles, and the concept of a built-in fashion obsolescence now seems dated. After all, everything good comes around again and again anyway, and the great, flattering, classic styles from every decade never

really go away at all. Because design snippets from six different decades now coexist beautifully in a single season, "retro" has ceased to have any meaning and "vintage" is only a matter of age. If a garment is well preserved, well designed, and well made, it can continue its life in any decade.

As designers began to see fashion as an ever-flowing river, always doubling back on itself, interest in its usable past began to grow. In particular, the 1973–1986 tenure of *Vogue* editor Diana Vreeland at New York's Costume Institute at the Metropolitan Museum of Art sparked a whole new attitude toward the preservation and study of the great clothes of earlier decades. With every well-mounted, highly publicized exhibition Vreeland dreamed up, appreciation grew. Important garments came to be seen as objects to be venerated, preserved, and collected—as the works of art that they were now perceived to be. In the vintage world, the trickle-down effect was slow but sure. It was during these decades that many antique dealers added vintage clothes to their stock, specialty vintage dealers opened their doors, and the auction houses of London and New York established their fashion departments. While some of their buyers were serious collectors of couture dresses and other fragile antique garments, increasingly they were also women who bought to wear.

Potential buyers who were put off by the idea of rooting around in musty thrift shops and campy boutiques soon discov-

ered that the vintage shopping experience was now much like any other—that they could expect clean, organized stock, attractive displays, dressing rooms, and helpful, knowledgeable staff. For those who don't need to browse in person, on-line services like eBay have added a whole other shopping dimension. Vintage buyers in every location—no matter how remote—now have access to huge numbers of offerings, while on-line databases provide useful information about where to shop in your area.

Of course the adventurous can still savor the joy of foraging in thrift stores, flea markets, jumble and resale shops. There are still plenty of finds waiting out there for the thrifty buyer who likes to tell about the time she found eight Mary Quant dresses, still wrapped in tissue, in the bottom of the box lot at Brimfield. Women are also sparking up their

individuality

wardrobes without laying out a single penny. Those fifteen-year-old jackets or dresses that seemed outdated but "too good to give away" are now coming out of the closet and being added to contemporary wardrobes with surprisingly powerful results.

But budget considerations no longer drive this market. Screen and fashion icons like Barbra Streisand, Winona Ryder, Demi Moore, Madonna, Ashley Judd, and others are frequently seen wearing vintage clothes. Since these women could obviously wear contemporary couture every day of the week, they are sending a powerful message: Vintage is no longer about making do. It's about having what nobody else can have—about looking wonderful while not looking like everybody else. "It's about hidden luxury, the stuff you don't see," says Annette Tapert, coauthor of *The Power of Style*. "The linings, the detailing, the tailoring. It's about workmanship. It's about the way it fits and the way it moves." Then Tapert adds: "Why would you buy a new Chanel when you can get the real things from the '60s for half the price?"

Contemporary clothes often have a cookie-cutter quality that doesn't suit today's sensibilities and, more important, the quality gap between today's ready-to-wear and that of the past is considerable. Even forty years ago, many noncouture clothes were still hand-sewn by "little dressmakers" using a wide range of fabrics no longer available. When you wear vintage, the shape of the garment may look much like the modern version, but the eye registers the difference—the draping, the fit, the hang simply cannot be duplicated.

But perhaps the most obvious advantage of wearing vintage is the ability to show yourself off to your best advantage. Not everyone is tall and model thin. If you are short-waisted, petite, long-legged, or anything else, there are classic styles out there that will make you look great. Designers may not provide these in any particular fashion year, but you can go out and get them for yourself. Vintage shoppers learn to pinpoint the decades in which the clothes best suit their particular figures, and to focus their shopping excursions accordingly. Some are '60s girls who collect Empire-waist dresses: others are leggy Katharine Hepburn types who go for '40s high-waisted trousers.

It's all out there, like a vast smorgasbord of style, ready and waiting to stretch your budget, brighten your contemporary wardrobe, and telegraph your personal style. In these pages, we'll tell you how to do it all: how to shop for vintage classics and how to wear them beautifully, everyday. Your fashion persona will never be the same.

The Clothes

See how easily classic vintage clothes add style and versatility to any wardrobe. On the following pages thirty-seven vintage garments are shown worn by women (and one man) of various ages, bodytypes, and professions. Each example is shown three different ways—incorporated into a casual, workday, and evening outfit that may include contemporary or other vintage pieces.

In a sidebar we've summarized the genesis, style, and history of the featured garment. If it was made by a known designer, we note it. Otherwise we list its silhouette, any detail that sets it apart, designers who were part of its history, and the fashionable people associated with it. It's all part of the special pleasure and interest of vintage clothes.

So get into vintage and have fun. You won't look like everyone else but you will look great.

Featured Designer André Courrèges
Silhouette Cropped
Detail Plastic zipper
History B. H. Wragge, Christian Dior, Pierre Cardin
Famous Amelia Earhart

The dashing young pilots of World War II didn't need long, bulky outerwear that would restrict their movements in the cockpit. They were the first to wear the "bomber" or "battle" jacket—a distinctive waist-length jacket with a fitted bottom—but hardly the last. Designers of the '60s like Courrèges, Cardin, and Dior were quick to adapt this silhouette for their sportswear lines, adding it to their roster of short, unfitted jackets (so flattering to those of us who are just a tad short-waisted) that made their appearance at mid-century and never went away.

Up until then women had been content with longer jackets that covered the hips, extremely short jackets (like the bolero), or very fitted styles, with a distinct waist. B. H. Wragge, an American sportswear designer favored by college girls, was the first out of the gate with a 1949 suit featuring a short, boxy jacket. His pioneering effort prefigured the waistless styles of the '50s and early '60s, including the short cardigan suit jackets Chanel featured at her February 1954 "comeback" show and the chunky, waist-length suit jackets worn by Jackie Kennedy as she campaigned with her husband in 1960. Both became instant fashion classics.

the 60s waist-length jacket

worn by Sloan, talk show host

Things got a little less ladylike in the mid–'60s when André Courrèges and others showed playful jackets in pastel colors and space-age materials that evoked the short, dashing bomber.

That's exactly what we have here. What could be more fun than this '60s pink plastic patent leather Courrèges number with white snaps up the front and on the cuffs? When Sloan wears her weekend uniform of white jeans and a T-shirt, she simply adds the jacket and suddenly looks completely pulled together.

For work, she creates her own modern version of the suit, pairing a white, pleated, stretch-nylon skirt with her pink jacket (very Courrèges, but black would do just as well—or how about chocolate brown?) and adding a funky pair of faux zebra open toes. Anybody can throw a pastel cashmere sweater over a little black dress in the evening, but this bomber jacket is much more fun. Fortunately, pairing two true classics almost always works.

Silhouette Form-fitting, high-necked
Detail Halter shape
History Football captains, submarine captains
Famous Greta Garbo, Noël Coward

the turtleneck sweater

worn by Elizabeth, journalist

"Turtleneck girl . . ." sings James Taylor in a song from the '80s. "Baby boom baby . . ." Actually, the turtleneck sweater goes back a bit further than that—to the 1860s in fact—when British athletes first incorporated high-necked, roll-over collar jerseys into their uniforms. By 1900 the turtleneck jersey had become part of American collegiate football gear, and shortly thereafter it was borrowed for the uniform of naval men who served aboard submarines. The reason for its amphibious name is obvious, but it is not clear who first used it, or when. Meanwhile, the turtleneck had made its way into the civilian population, where it became many things to many people. Noël Coward made it the ultimate in chic with a blazer while Greta Garbo immortalized it

90s

"The turtleneck is a venerable classic that will enhance any wardrobe."

70s

23.

as part of the tweedy '40s menswear look. Beatniks of the '50s thought it was "Cool daddy-o," and it soon became part of the no-shirt-and-tie "leisure" look that swept the nation in the '70s.

After that the turtleneck was everywhere. A slim-fitting version dominated the '80s, while the outdoors look of catalog companies like Eddie Bauer and Land's End made it the ubiquitous garb of the early '90s. Fashion pundits dubbed 1996 "the year of the turtleneck," but they could have been talking about any year since 1970. Warm, flattering, and the perfect way to emphasize a long, slender neck (or hide a sagging chin), the turtleneck is a venerable classic that will enhance any wardrobe.

Elizabeth's sexy halter-neck version isn't very old—it was made about 1990—but it could have been made in 1970 or 1950. Pale lavender cashmere, it's the perfect counterpoint to her '70s bell-bottoms in navy/white narrow whale corduroy. The sleek top emphasizes Elizabeth's toned upper body and is nicely balanced by the sweep of bell-bottom material below. For her workday Elizabeth goes for straight-legged khakis and a leather jacket in the same color as the sweater. The jacket hides the sweater's bareness and pulls her look together. By night the bareness is back. Elizabeth wears her halter with a skirt made of a thick lavender satin decorated with starbursts of sequins. The skirt is new, but the fabric dates back to the mid-'70s and was used because the designer liked it better than anything out there today. Elizabeth's strappy shoes are also from the '70s, as are her disco earrings. Her hairstylist boyfriend has done her hair in pigtails, giving her the mischievous look of a schoolgirl grown up—a turtleneck girl with a sense of humor. It looks like she's about to have a lot of fun.

Featured Designer Giorgio di Sant'Angelo
Silhouette Hugs the body
Detail changes shape
History Claire McCardell
Famous Donna Karan

the bodysuit

worn by Stephanie, communications specialist

70s

It is said that the fastidious Duke of Windsor, not wishing his shirt to become loose from his trousers, concocted a way to attach it to his undergarments—thus inventing the first body-suit. However, this was not an innovation the Duke cared to claim and so many people now believe that Donna Karan first came up with that sleek, one-piece garment that starts between our legs and makes its way up from there. Whatever. The concept was certainly familiar to every "bal-let beatnik" of the '50s who mooched around in a leotard in an effort to look as if she had just left dance practice, and to American designer Claire McCardell, whose wrapped bathing suits of the '40s and '50s look an awful lot like bodysuits. It was McCardell who first championed the idea of a garment that takes on the shape of the wearer—not vice versa.

Body-conscious clothes were de rigueur for the aerobics queens of the '70s and '80s who worked out hard and wanted everybody to know it. It was the age of Lycra, spandex, and other stretchy, shiny synthetics—perfect for roller disco and skateboarding, not to mention those endless aerobics classes. Enter designer Giorgio di Sant'Angelo, who in the '70s took the bodysuit to a whole new place and created a new fashion classic. Sant'Angelo made versatile, stretchy pieces—an entire, packable wardrobe for the modern woman. A single Lycra tube, for example, could be a dress or just a top, depending on how far up you pulled. His materials were beautiful, his colors memorable; these instant classics are sought after by collectors as well as wearers and are featured at auctions and vintage stores.

Stephanie's example is actually a bathing suit (shades of Claire McCardell) from the early '70s, in dazzling aqua Lycra. It's almost formless until you have it on, and then nothing could be sexier. For the beach, Stephanie has wrapped it so that it bares her navel and skims her shoulders, crossing over her breasts. It looks great with a pair of airy crocheted wool bell-bottom pants of the same date—very Saint-Tropez. For her workday, the same bodysuit becomes a demure halter, adding a splash of color to a contemporary black pantsuit, staying in the background—as versatile as a shell or tank. When night falls, however, the same bodysuit becomes a classic, shapely, shoulder-baring bodice—sheer glamour when worn with this rustling silk taffeta evening skirt in hot pink. Who ever said pink and blue was boring?

"Who ever said pink and blue was boring?"

Silhouette A-line mini

Detail Industrial material

History Mary Quant, André Courrèges, Pierre Cardin

Famous Goldie Hawn, Twiggy

the mini-skirt

worn by Lisa, mergers and acquisitions lawyer

Like all great ideas, the miniskirt is an innovation for which many people are happy to take credit. The question has even taken on nationalistic tones: the French claim that André Courrèges was the first to raise hemlines; the English insist that their own Mary Quant was the true mother of this fashion revolution. Quant herself dismisses the whole thing, saying: "It was the girl in the street who invented it." However the style began, by the mid-'60s designers on both sides of the Channel were showing blatantly youth-oriented, thigh-high skirts—briefer than any seen before, and then some. Hemlines continued to rise, culminating in the ultrashort micro-minis of the late '60s. The silhouette was slightly flared; fabrics were often stiff and colors bright. "Space-age" plastics and technological details like large zippers were popular. Gabrielle Chanel pronounced the new fashion "disgusting."

But everyone else loved it. When in 1965 the first group of miniskirted British models arrived in New York City, they literally stopped traffic. Here were clothes clearly different from anything one's mother had ever worn. What freedom! What a way to proclaim the glory of one's youth! There were a few attendant difficulties, of course, but modeling and finishing schools simply instructed their charges in the proper way to get in and out of low sportscars and everybody went merrily on—until the early '70s. By then designers had introduced the "maxi" skirt and although not everybody cheered, hemlines were definitely on the way down. But by the mid-'80s they were back—no longer revolutionary but perfect for the youthful,

80s

"the rich gypsy look"

peared during World War II, only to return with a vengeance in Christian Dior's "New Look" of 1947. By then everyone was starved for an opulent, feminine silhouette and the princess skirt certainly fit the bill. Throughout the late '40s and '50s the shape was worn by everybody from a customer of couture to a teenager on a date in Akron, Ohio—not to mention every bride. In the '80s it was worn by a real princess bride—Princess Diana—and soon was back in fashion across the board. Vivienne Westwood used it in a 1988 corset-top dress, and Donna Karan created a short dress with a princess skirt made out of hot pink scuba-diving material. Classic doesn't mean old-fashioned. This silhouette is as timeless as you can get and it looks good on almost everyone.

Marina looks fabulous in an organza and tulle Carolyne Roehm princess skirt from the late '80s. For a morning's shopping in a resort town she throws on a white T-shirt and knots a denim shirt ('70s, bought at the Rose Ball flea market in L.A.) at her waist. The taupe skirt quiets down and goes a little funky—the rich gypsy look—especially when worn with chunky jewelry and plastic sandals.

60s

On assignment for an article on fashion, Marina needs to stand out and show her style: She puts on a tank cut like a child's T-shirt and tops it with a gold-toned chain bolero trimmed with fringe and faux crystal beads from the early '60s. All of the gold and taupe tones work together, while high heels lift the skirt to ankle length. When evening comes Marina wears a strapless bustier top she had made adorned with Carolyne Roehm's shells and silk flowers. Suddenly you notice that the skirt is embroidered in gold and copper thread and that the underskirt is peach tulle. The subtle colors, the strapless bodice, the delicate flowers, the long graceful lines of the skirt—no fairy godmother could have done better by this princess.

"Classic doesn't mean old-fashioned."

Featured Designer Oscar de la Renta
Silhouette A-line
Detail Ottoman silk
History Christian Dior, Charles Frederick Worth, Cristóbal Balenciaga, Oleg Cassini
Famous Jackie O, Audrey Hepburn

the princess dress

worn by Su-Lin, news producer

The princess dress is the ultimate classic silhouette and it has the pedigree to prove it. It started with a real royal—the French Empress Eugénie, the greatest style leader of the Second Empire. Enter the greatest couturier of that day—Charles Frederick Worth, a talented, enterprising Englishman who had set up shop in Paris in the late 1850s. Soon he was dressing everybody who was anybody, including Eugénie. By 1864 Worth had over one thousand employees and the Empress had inaugurated a new style in her elegant Worth gowns—flat in the front and slightly gathered in the back.

Christian Dior, the greatest couturier of his day, must have been rooting around in 19th-century French history when he christened his 1951 silhouette "The Princess Line." His dresses were a considerably updated version of Worth's—fitted through the midriff, but leaving the waist

60s

unmarked. This flattering line was accomplished with the use of six panels of fabric, from shoulders to hem. The style was nothing less than an instant hit, and other designers soon picked it up. On this side of the Atlantic, Pauline Trigère became known as the "mistress of the princess cut," and in the early '60s, Oleg Cassini designed many of Jacqueline Kennedy's influential dresses in the same lovely, classic style. Since then the princess line has been done by almost everybody, in almost every decade. Think Bill Blass, Oscar de la Renta, Ralph Lauren, Tuleh. Think flattering, ladylike, but never dull. Think like a princess and try this silhouette.

Su-Lin did. She got this '80s (could have been '60s or '50s), red silk taffeta Oscar de la Renta off-the-rack dress at a sample sale for a ridiculously low price and then discovered that it is versatile as well as beautiful. When she wears it under a '60s plastic trench coat with an Op Art pattern in the same red, a nylon backpack, and a pair of '70s sunglasses she picked up at a flea market, it becomes part of a casual outfit, perfect for a week-end movie. Back at work on Monday, the dress becomes a skirt beneath a man's '50s shirt tied around her waist. A scarf completes a traditional, professional look. When evening comes, Su-Lin unties her shirt, steps into a pair of contemporary mules, and picks up her '60s red bag. If she's meeting her elderly aunt for dinner she will be perfectly dressed, and a younger crowd will immediately pick up on the hip, retro aspects of her choice. Ladylike can be sexy.

50s

39.

80s

Featured Designer Emilio Pucci
Silhouette One piece
Detail Bright, graphic print
History Pierre Cardin, André Courrèges, Norman
Norell, Geoffrey Beene
Famous Barbarella, Elizabeth Hurley

60s

the jumpsuit

worn by Vanessa, PR executive

Everyone knows a Pucci print when they see one, but few are aware that the man behind the magic was Emilio Pucci—an Italian marchese from an aristocratic Florentine family who competed on the Italian national ski team and was a flying ace in World War II. After the war this Renaissance man happened to design some forward-looking skiwear for himself and his chums and the rest is history. In the years that followed Pucci became known as the "Prince of Prints," drawing on classic patterns like hieroglyphics, Sicilian carts, Doric columns, and heraldic devices from Siena's Palio to create a new kind of clothing. It was made of colorful silk, cotton, or synthetic jersey— light and packable. The shapes were simple and didn't change much from season to season, and with their clear association with the jet set aristocracy and their Mediterranean haunts, they were always in fashion. It was a simple idea that took the world by storm.

In 1961, inspired by the Space Race and NASA, Pucci began to make one-piece "cat suits" or "jumpsuits" for after-ski. This one-piece garment was already familiar to Pucci as the uniform of fly- ers and parachute jumpers in World War II. (It had, in fact, served the same purpose during World War I.) It was a silhouette he was to use well into the '70s for leisure wear of all kinds. Other designers also appreciated the garment's space-age associations and sleek design possibili- ties: Pierre Cardin, André Courrèges, Norman Norell, Anne Klein, and Geoffrey Beene all showed versions of the jumpsuit throughout the '60s and '70s. Many, like this example from the mid-'60s, featured flowing palazzo pants. Others were more closely fitted or sported sleeveless overcoats. Jumpsuits were worn everywhere— from the beach to the ballroom—until they morphed into more athletic-looking "bodysuits" in the spandex-crazy '80s.

Vanessa found this example at a Los Angeles vin- tage store, where she had to move fast to snag it. Everybody is looking for Pucci these days. It's made of silk jersey with a zipper back and a high waist, fitted through the midriff, in one of Pucci's "warm" color palettes, including a lot of hot pink. In thirty years nothing has changed. Anything by Pucci still looks perfect and this jumpsuit is great all by itself—ready for any casual occasion. For a day at work, Vanessa slips into high suede pumps and flings on a Christian Dior khaki car coat from the '50s. A pink scarf echoes one of Pucci's colors. It's a more covered-up look, but still a knockout for any fashion-conscious office. That night, the jumpsuit becomes a pair of flowing evening trousers, topped with a slimming '50s black cash- mere sweater. Its off-the-shoulder neckline and fitted waist are super-flattering to all but the very low-waisted. Pucci and a little black sweater— forever fashionable.

50s

"Pucci and a little black sweater—
forever fashionable."

Silhouette To the waist

Detail Two coordinating pieces

History Gabrielle Chanel, Jean Patou,
Bill Blass, Halston

Famous Lana Turner

50s

the sweater set

worn by Holly, editor

"Before Gabrielle Chanel," wrote one fashion historian, "sweaters had been the province of old ladies, school children, and fishermen." Not a very fashion-forward group. But thanks to Chanel—and her archrival Jean Patou—by the end of the '20s sweaters had become very stylish indeed. In that decade Chanel introduced the knit suit and the knit cardigan jacket for both resort and city dressing, and Patou did something new and rather interesting: He began to show shells and long cardigans in sophisticated, modernistic patterns that "read" only if the two pieces were worn together. These were the first examples of the classic silhouette known as the "sweater set" or "twinset."

By the end of the '30s the twinset had developed a new and very definite personality. Shorter and perkier, it was a practical, no-nonsense, all-American look, perfect for a wartime wardrobe. It didn't hurt that movie stars like Rita Hayworth and Lana Turner were frequently photographed in sweater sets. Demure yet clinging, this silhouette allowed these pinup girls to be "America's sweet-hearts" and sexy "sweater girls" at the same time. Not a bad trick. In postwar America sexiness was toned down considerably and the twinset became the symbol of suburban housewifely correctness and—collected in as many cashmere colors as possible—the ultimate teenage status object. As often happens in fashion, the wheel turns and one is back where one started: Like the long-ago knits of Chanel and Patou, the sweater set is just itself again—as attractive and versatile as ever—done in every recent decade by designers like Tse, Bill Blass, Marc Jacobs, and Adrienne Vittadini.

It would be impossible to guess in what decade Holly's example was made, so we'll tell you: the '50s. (You could get the same thing at the Gap, but the cashmere would be thinner, the shaping less interesting, the color less beautifully baby blue.) She wears her long-sleeved shell on the weekends with a pair of khaki pants and ties her cardigan around her waist. It's a look that hasn't failed in fifty years and it never will.

"Before Gabrielle Chanel, sweaters had been the province of old ladies."

Putting on her sweater, substituting black pants for the khakis and adding a strand of pearls, Holly is ready for work. Her outfit, in the great American tradition of sportswear-in-the-mainstream, would be right for all but the most formal of offices.

Black and blue is so chic at night. Holly throws her baby blue cardigan over her sexy black evening dress and puts on a pair of baby blue pumps. The sweater is as successful an "accent" as any shawl and much more interesting. She looks comfortable, confident, and still formally dressed. It's an evening look that Halston, Calvin Klein, Anne Klein, and Donna Karan have done to perfection. All you need is one half of a sweater set.

Featured Designer Missoni
Silhouette Trapeze
Detail Piping
History Gabrielle Chanel, Redfern,
Christian Dior, Yves Saint Laurent
Famous Lisa Fonssagrives

60s

the suit— skirt and jacket

worn by Emmanuelle, retail executive

We don't usually think of the ladies of the Edwardian era as "New Women" but that's exactly what they called themselves. They were claiming freedoms and rights their mothers had never dreamed of (going out to work, riding a bicycle) and they wanted to dress the part. Enter a British tailor called Redfern who created a jacket and skirt ensemble using the same materials and craftsmanship heretofore reserved for men's suits. By the turn of the century "tailormades" as these outfits were called, were everywhere—taking women of leisure through their entire day (a novel idea in an era when ladies changed for each new event) and providing practical garb for the hordes of women entering the workforce.

By the '20s the suit was no longer just a utilitarian tweed uniform: It had become a staple of American fashion, as sensitive to changes in shape and style as the day dress or evening gown. Accordingly, jackets were longer and skirts shorter in the '20s, and shapes were more romantic and fluid in the '30s. Wartime restrictions made early '40s suits plainer and shorter, while the New Look drowned them in feminine yardage. The list goes on, covering the boxy "Jackie O" styles of the early '60s and the big-shouldered "power" suits of the '80s. Only Gabrielle Chanel remained true to a single vision: a classic, unchanging cardigan jacket and simple, straight skirt, from the '20s, through the '50s and beyond. For some it's still The Suit, and always will be.

Emmanuelle's suit is a classic in its own right. It was made in the '60s with a modified tent back silhouette and a straight, knee-length skirt. The tent back made its appearance in the '40s, dominated the '50s along with the other loose-fitting shapes pioneered by Dior and Saint Laurent, and was reprised in the '90s. Here, the material is plastic patent leather—an early example of the "space-age" materials of the '60s—but the color,

"shiny, funky plastic"

70s

the elegant tent back silhouette, and the unusual three-quarter sleeves make it a natural for an evening out, especially when paired with pink satin and faux leopard Mary Janes designed by Emmanuelle herself and a bag she found to match. For daytime wear, Emmanuelle creates an unmatched suit—substituting a demure ca. 1956 ivory wool double-breasted jacket with now impossible-to-get jaguar collar and cuffs and leather buttons. For an even more casual look, Emmanuelle wears her shiny, funky plastic skirt with a openwork striped Missoni knit turtleneck from the '70s (modestly backed with a bodysuit) and carries a '70s plastic magazine clutch bag.

50s

Featured Designer Christian Dior
Silhouette "Y" line detail, knife pleats
History Jean Patou, Gabrielle Chanel,
Elsa Schiaparelli
Famous White tennis dress
worn by Suzanne Lenglen in 1921

the dress
and jacket

worn by Gale, fashion and beauty entrepreneur

Why would a woman who could have anything she wants wear a forty-five-year-old suit? Perhaps because, as an expert on beauty and fashion, she knows a winner when she sees one. When Gale saw this 1955 Christian Dior dress and jacket in oatmeal linen—the sleeveless dress low in the torso above a knife-pleated skirt, the short jacket fitted and single-breasted—she knew it would be a worthy acquisition to an already stellar wardrobe. "It's all about quality," she says simply. "This kind of fabric and workmanship simply isn't available anymore. The suit looks as good today as the day it was made. I don't think of it as vintage." She continues, "I think of it as something great that fills a hole in my wardrobe. It's unique, beautiful, flattering—and versatile. I can even wear the jacket with jeans."

The origins of this classic silhouette are equally casual and can be dated to 1921 when French tennis champion Suzanne Lenglen bounded onto the court in a white dress designed by couturier Jean Patou. Its simple bodice and knife-pleated skirt—cut daringly, just below the knee—allowed freedom of movement and emphasized the wearer's lithe, youthful form. It was a style that was to dominate the '20s—popularized by Patou, Gabrielle Chanel, and others who understood that women needed clothes for their new, active, less formal lifestyle. In this decade too, Chanel first pioneered the use of natural colors like this suit's subtle gray-beige. Elsa Schiaparelli—her greatest rival—introduced the now-classic formula of dress and matching jacket, sometime in the '30s.

50s

Christian Dior drew on all of this fashion history when he created his great suits of the late '40s and '50s. His voluminous, shaped "New Look" of 1947 had thrilled a postwar world starved for luxury and femininity, but by 1955 he had refined his silhouette, producing clothes with more ease and less fabric. The dress and jacket are an example of his "Y" line of that year, which gracefully skimmed the waist and featured a lengthened torso. The crispness and precision of Dior's knife pleats add greatly to the look. They were produced by choosing a pleat-friendly fabric like linen and sewing rows of horizontal tacking stitches on their underside.

The fitted, perfectly tailored jacket is itself a neutral staple that mixes well with these gray wool trousers, for a casual Saturday shopping excursion. Pale golf shoes echo its color and pull together the look. The dress and jacket are the perfect workday duo—covered up and businesslike but unmistakably elegant. When Gale removes the jacket, the sleeveless, gracefully fitted dress needs only a pair of high heels, gloves, and more formal jewelry to make it the perfect day-into-night choice.

55.

"I don't think of it as vintage."

Featured Designers Ralph Lauren, Pierre Cardin
Silhouette Masculine
Detail Nipped waist
History Gabrielle Chanel, Yves Saint Laurent,
Bill Blass, Giorgio Armani
Famous Lauren Hutton

The double-breasted jacket is a blatant—and very successful—borrowing from menswear. Seeking more freedom of movement and simplicity in dress, late 19th-century women began sporting "tailormade" suits (jackets and skirts) in materials, style, and workmanship similar to their menfolk's. These "tailored" jackets were always part of a suit and were cut in the distinctive "S" silhouette of the Edwardian era (puffed out in front and behind, with a small waist in the center). It took the inimitable Gabrielle Chanel to adapt the sporty, modern cut of menswear (including sailors' pea coats) to women's fashions and, in the late teens, to create the first jackets we would recognize as a "blazer." Long, lean jackets like this one exactly suited the straight boyish silhouette of the '20s and were worn with contrasting skirts or trousers right through the '30s, in both single- and double-breasted styles. Blazers continued to be worn in the '40s—although wartime restrictions on fabric made them shorter—but the '50s favored nipped waists and boxier styles.

By 1962 the long blazer was back—reprised by Yves Saint Laurent—and it has never been out of fashion since. Long, short, double- or single-breasted, the blazer became the single most important article of clothing of the '70s—with examples created by designers from Calvin Klein to Perry Ellis. Women were pouring into the workforce and the blazer became their uniform of choice. Its similarity to those worn by men made it the symbol of equality and proclaimed the wearer to be a serious contender. In the decades that followed the blazer lost its symbolic status but gained a permanent niche among fashion classics. It remains an indispensable part of every woman's wardrobe.

This example came from Ralph Lauren in the early '90s, but it might have been made anytime

long double

60s

breasted blazer

worn by Pamela, cyberspace entrepreneur

60s

in the last thirty years. It's every inch a classic—
black crepe with a long, lean cut that emphasizes
the length of Pamela's legs and gives everything
she wears a clean, pulled-together look. White
pleather (plastic leather) stretch pants from the
'80s and a '60s British flag T-shirt bought at a
secondhand shop on the King's Road might be a
bit kitschy and flashy on their own. But add a
black tailored blazer and suddenly it all works.
When it's time to go to the office, Pamela's blazer
is in its element. She pairs it with a white T-shirt
and a '60s Pierre Cardin off-the-rack, cotton knit
skirt in a swirling Op Art print. Professional, but
very cool. Because it's black crepe, the same blazer
makes the transition to evening with ease. Here it
tops a black lace slip from the '30s (purchased on-
line for $30), forming a single, slim black column
that flatters any figure. A pashmina in a caramel
color softens the blazer's tailored lines and provides a needed spot of color.

"Suddenly it all works."

30s

Featured Designer André Courrèges
Silhouette Tunic
Detail Faux vest
History Hattie Carnegie, Rudi Gernreich, Claire McCardell
Famous Peggy Moffat, Twiggy

the jumper

worn by Michelle, graduate student

The jumper is an inherently young silhouette and there's not a thing wrong with looking young. It's been worn in every decade of the 20th century, effortlessly dressed up or down, alternately making the wearer appear as wholesome as Heidi, or as "come hither" as Lolita. If we seem to be using a lot of schoolgirl similes, that's because the jumper has its roots firmly in the school yard—or at least the gymnasium. Its first incarnation was as a late 19th-century "exercise" suit for the young lady. Its practicality (you could launder just the cotton blouse underneath and call it a day) also made it the perfect school uniform—a use that continues today.

Meanwhile, designers quickly caught on to the jumper's fashion appeal. The '20s and '30s favored pinafore styles, often used for "playclothes" but by the '40s and '50s the jumper was just as popular for street wear by day and night. College girls chose B. H. Wragge jumpers for class and black velveteen jumpers with white organdy blouses for Saturday-night dates. Anne Fogarty showed a black corduroy jumper with a pale blue poplin shirt and Hattie Carnegie took the style downtown, pairing a black sequined jumper with a lace-trimmed organdy blouse. In the coffeehouses

61.

60s

60s

beatniks wore a virtual uniform of gray wool jumpers over black turtlenecks and tights. The '60s were all about youth and the jumper was everywhere—used by Pierre Cardin, André Courrèges, and Madame Grès, just to name a few. In the '70s, '80s, '90s, and beyond, the jumper has continued to be an appealing option—shown by designers as diverse as Geoffrey Beene and Giorgio di Sant'Angelo.

Michelle's '60s André Courrèges windowpane-checked wool jumper manages to be both collegiate and sexy. Made of a classic menswear fabric, it nevertheless leaves no doubt that the wearer is a girl—and a sophisticated one at that. Its illusion of an attached "vest" harks back to that most sophisticated of designers—Elsa Schiaparelli— and her famous 1930 sweater with the "bow" knitted right into the material. It's also extremely well made in a particularly densely woven wool. Try finding that kind of fabric and tailoring today for a price any sane person can afford. Michelle wears it on the weekends under a forest green pea coat purchased at a vintage show for $40. Worn open, the coat makes a fine cardigan for fall or spring. For a day of teaching, Michelle wears high leather boots and brings out the colors in her jumper with a '70s wool Italian bodysuit. Worn with nothing underneath, the jumper becomes a classic sleeveless A-line dress—perfect for an evening at a restaurant. A '50s handbag and vintage pumps complete the look.

Silhouette Straight
Detail Pin-striped
History Yves Saint Laurent, Emilio Pucci,
André Courrèges
Famous Audrey Hepburn

straight pants

worn by Lauren, fashion historian

The '50s was the first decade to take its fashion cues from teenage street style, and it was during these years that the slim, straight, "cigarette" or "stovepipe" trouser was born. It was a bold, body-conscious shape designed to separate this new generation from the previous one and the dismal wartime years. No more pleats, bags, or cuffs. No more overalls. It was time to rock and roll. Young American men, firmly under the spell of James Dean and Elvis Presley, were suddenly wearing skintight pants and pointy winkle-picker shoes. Even those rival British gangs, the "Mods" and "Rockers," agreed that when it came to one's trousers, straight and tight was the way to go. Meanwhile, the more cerebral element known as "beatniks" were devoted to a similar silhouette they called "student's pants." Think Audrey Hepburn in *Funny Face*—those straight black pants, ballet flats, and gamine haircut. A great look for any decade.

The fashion establishment soon jumped on the bandwagon. Trousers were not yet accepted for formal day wear in the '50s, but they were increasingly important to evening and casual collections and many designers were attracted to this young, ultrafeminine silhouette. In particular,

Yves Saint Laurent and Emilio Pucci popularized the straight, slim shape and made it the look for '50s pants. Youthfulness took on even more importance in the Swinging Sixties and the cigarette pant endured. In 1964 it was taken up by André Courrèges whose pantsuits were soon being worn by women for all occasions. Although pants widened out during the late '60s and '70s, the straight, slim pant—now a fashion classic—reappeared in the late '80s and has stayed on the scene. It will be with us forever.

Lauren found these '60s black pin-striped beauties in a thrift shop and she hasn't had them off since. "These pants can take me anywhere. They are effortless and have such a clean line. All I have to do is add a little something to jazz up my look." On a casual day, Lauren pairs her lean black pants with a bright contemporary tank top and vintage blue 1970 Nikes, which she discovered being sold as "extra stock" in a flea market for $14.

Lauren attends class in the same pants and a black '70s rib knit turtleneck sweater but punches up her outfit by adding a pair of sexy red heels. For an easy evening look, she simply removes the sweater and slips into a late '50s V-necked top—a vintage store find—in blazing red crepe adorned with hot pink sequins. The top may be worn at its original waist length or tucked under to show the wearer's midriff.

"These pants can take me anywhere."

50s

Featured Designer Karl Lagerfeld for Chanel

Silhouette Corsetlike

Detail Boning

History Christian Dior, Cristóbal Balenciaga, Pierre Balmain, Jean-Paul Gaultier, Vivienne Westwood

Famous Madonna

the bustier

worn by Kalliope, bon vivant

The official definition—a strapless, one-piece support garment—doesn't begin to convey the allure of the bustier. It's a sexy, flattering, surprisingly versatile little item that everybody should consider. Don't just think Madonna in the '80s—think Dior in the '50s. This is a classic that's been around for a long, long time. Although the term "bustier" wasn't yet used by designers, every strapless dress from the '30s and '40s had a boned or otherwise carefully constructed bodice that kept its contents firmly in place. In the late '40s, designers began to play with the idea of a strapless bodice that looked like a real corset—the bustier's utilitarian 19th-century forebear. Dior himself did a bustier dress in 1949, and in 1950 English designer Hardy Amies showed a swathed silk skirt topped with a strapless lace "corselet." One year later Pierre Balmain went all the way with his taffeta and velvet "corset" evening dress with obvious corset stitching.

In the late '80s it was déjà vu all over again. Madonna sported that famous-flesh colored number with the pointy seamed cups and Jean-Paul Gaultier showed even more extreme versions of the same. Designers like John Anthony were making evening dresses with tight, sleek bustier bodices. As style makers had done forty years before, Vivienne Westwood and Karl Lagerfeld for Chanel took their inspiration directly from the bustier corset, molding the super-fit bodies of that era in silver lace and supple leather. Women also discovered that the silhouette was dynamite under a jacket—a modern version of a camisole—but sleeker and more romantic.

50s

Silhouette Tapered
Detail Slits at bottom
History Emilio Pucci, Yves Saint Laurent
Famous Sophia Loren, Marilyn Monroe

capri pants

worn by Debbie,
museum executive

50s

At the mere mention of "capri pants," you'll immediately picture a terrace on the Riviera and a stunning Italian starlet in sunglasses, a halter top, and, of course, slim, tight pants that end just below the knee in a seductive split. That's because during the '50s—when this silhouette made its first appearance—the outdoor, bohemian chic of films like *The Barefoot Contessa* was having a huge influence on fashion. So was the work of Emilio Pucci, who is said to have coined the term "capri pants" in the first place. Apparently the designer-count was having an affair with a beautiful woman on that Mediterranean island and decided to name the silhouette he was to use so often in his resort collections after the scene of his latest rendezvous.

If the capri pant was the uniform of the European jet set of the '50s and early '60s, in America it was adopted by two very different constituencies—the student population known as "beatniks" (always in coffeehouse black) and the suburban mom (never in black). After a few years out of the limelight, the silhouette returned to prominence in the '80s, popularized by Madonna and other fashion-forward rock and rollers. The slim, tight capri was a natural for that body-obsessed era, and the shape's association with iconic figures like Brigitte Bardot and Sophia Loren didn't hurt either. By the '90s, however, such associations

"Very Ann-Margret."

were just frosting on the cake: Flattering, versatile, and sexy, capri pants had passed into the realm of the classic where they remain until this day.

Capris are perfect for Debbie, accentuating as they do her narrow hips and slender legs. On the weekends she throws on this pair in black cotton denim from the mid–'50s and tops it with her husband's '70s brown suede hunting shirt. Costume jewelry from an '80s runway show and a pair of ballet flats finish the look. Her outfit is comfortable but very Audrey Hepburn—a more put-together version of the ubiquitous leggings-and- big-shirt. For a workday Debbie takes a unified approach— wearing her capris with a '50s double- breasted wool jacket in the same black. The pony- skin collar, stamped to look like leopard, adds interest, while the jacket's fine construction and lining give her a professional, tailored appearance. When night falls, Debbie changes gears again, putting on a silk jersey tank and topping it with a long, mandarin-collared jacket in linen and straw in a wicker pattern—an unusual blend of materials typical of its decade, the '50s. The black and white coloration is subtle, the jacket length elegant, and as these pictures make abundantly clear, capri pants are dynamite with high heels.

50s

Silhouette A line
Detail Velvet bows on lining, hidden pockets
History Military uniforms, motoring "dusters"
Famous Napoléon Bonaparte

the double-breasted coat

worn by
Shannon,
fashion
designer

Our first images of the double-breasted coat are exclusively military—British soldiers attacking the upstart American colonists in their double-breasted red coats and late–18th-century French officers parading in their double-breasted blue ones. There were reasons why soldiers of that era favored this style: It added an extra layer of warmth and, more important, protection. It was harder to stab somebody through that second layer of thick woolen fabric. That extra row of buttons buttoned from the left, of course, because then a man's right hand was free to hold his rifle. (Women's clothes button the opposite way to facilitate breast-feeding.) The pea coat is perhaps the best known 20th-century version of double-breasted naval garb.

The style quickly spread to the male civilian population, appearing in the late 18th century as the gentleman's "redingote," a triple-collared double-breasted coat with wide lapels, and in the late 19th century as the "ulster", a double-breasted woolen coat with a high button collar and half belt. Women were also getting into the act, and by 1904 "The Amazon," a long double-breasted motoring coat, provided warmth and protection in a new world. In the century that followed, the double-breasted silhouette has been used repeatedly in every single decade, changing its shape to conform to the prevailing fashion but never going out of style.

Shannon found this '60s natural mink coat with classic pea coat styling in a Palm Beach thrift store. The price was $200—less than what she

60s

"The fur was beautiful, and I knew I

would pay for a medium-priced cloth coat. "The fur was beautiful, and I knew I could wear it over everything from jeans to a little black dress," she says. "I love the maker's attention to detail. For example, there is a ribbon of velvet with little bows attached all around the beautiful satin lining and the buttons are handmade of glass beads." For a casual occasion Shannon wears a pair of '70s suede, fringed "cowboy" pants, a man's pigskin vest of the same date and '70s Frye boots— another thrift store find. When she adds the mink, "suddenly this ladylike coat is part of a rock and roll image." For work, the coat looks completely professional again, worn over a classic wool shift dress and cashmere cardigan, and in the evening, mink is, well, mink. It's the perfect complement to a black, sleeveless, wool shantung Empire-style dress of Shannon's own design. The similar hemlines give her a streamlined look and high-heeled calfskin boots keep everything young and modern.

could wear it over everything from jeans to a little black dress."

Featured Designer Jeanne Lanvin

Silhouette Wraps the body

Detail Brocade trim

History Claire McCardell, Joset Walker

Famous Joan Baez, Barbara Hutton

the drawstring skirt

worn by Ranya, Ph.D. student

There's a lot to be said for simplicity, and what could be simpler than the drawstring tie? It's just a slim scrap of fabric threaded through the top of a garment. When pulled it "draws" that garment in, in a most practical and attractive way. It's been a staple of Asian costume for centuries. (When was the last time you saw a button or belt buckle on a pair of filmy Indian trousers?) It is in fact, as simple and effective as a Japanese painting. Because the drawstring is made of the same fabric as the garment, that garment appears to have no closure apparatus at all to mar its lines. It magically gathers and shapes itself as the drawstring does its work.

This idea appealed mightily to designer Claire McCardell, who in the '40s, '50s and '60s utilized the drawstring tie on so many of her clothes.

McCardell, that most American of thinkers, liked the drawstring's implicit message: Every bit of material was being used in the production of a dress, making it an economical and streamlined operation. Joset Walker had another reason for her drawstring-waisted dresses of the '40s: They were easy to launder and iron—perfect for wartime. Both designers also may have been influenced by the abundance of drawstrings on early 20th–century lingerie. Before 1920 almost every corset cover, camisole, and pair of knickers sported one of these practical closures. Designers of the '70s were more interested in the mysterious East than vintage underwear, producing a host of Eastern-inspired drawstring trousers, skirts, and bloused peasant shirts with drawstring necklines.

50s

Featured Designer André Courrèges
Silhouette Low-riding
Detail Inner corseting
History Mary Quant, Betsey Johnson
Famous Brigitte Bardot

60s
69

The hourglass look is all very well, but there is something incredibly sexy about the low-slung, or hipster, silhouette. Designer Paul Poiret was one of the first to figure this out. Around 1918 he dropped the "waistline" to the hips and there it remained throughout the '20s. Forty years later when designers like Mary Quant, Betsey Johnson, and André Courrèges turned their focus to pants, they took their cue from button-front sailor pants, low-slung cowboy jeans, and harem pants. The hip-hugging pant dominated the '60s and beyond. Yves Saint Laurent's harem collection of 1973 also made good use of that sexy silhouette, as did other '70s designers and those of the late '90s.

Courrèges was the first to pair hip-hugging trousers with a matching top or jacket and so create a "pantsuit" suitable for professional or formal occasions. But it was still early in the revolution: In 1964 a pants-wearing socialite showed up for lunch at one of New York's best restaurants wearing a dressy pantsuit and the maître d' refused to seat her. (She simply removed her pants and lunched in her mini-length jacket.) Slowly, pants dressing gained acceptance until the late '60s when confusion and annoyance over changing hemlines (maxi or mini?) accelerated the process. By the early '70s the nation was in the throes of pantsuit mania and a fashionable woman could boast that she owned not a single skirt. Today's woman takes a more eclectic approach, but the pantsuit remains an important element of her wardrobe.

the

hipster

worn by Jennifer,
art dealer

pant

40s

Jennifer's suit is truly a classic—a black stretch
wool Courrèges design with flared, hip-hugging
trousers and matching jumper vest. Beautifully
made and lined, the corsetlike top and structured
trousers give her a long, lean, shapely line. For
weekend shopping Jennifer wears a contemporary
red plaid turtleneck under her black vest—an
unexpected choice that pairs two very different
classics. Pointy shoes complete her fashionable,
yet funky getup. Come Monday morning Jennifer
needs to lose the funk: Her fitted '40s riding
jacket echoes the flaring lines of the Courrèges
vest, while the red wool, crisp, white button-
down shirt, and silk scarf give her a professional
look. Jennifer's choice for evening is yet another
version of the original Courrèges concept but this
time the slightly flared, hip-length top is a fabulous sequined chiffon blouse from the late '20s
with a Peter Pan collar and ruffled front. The hip-
hugging pant continues to do its job—giving her
a sleek, curvy shape—without calling attention to
itself. Her silk envelope bag is also from the '20s.
Her look—timeless.

20s

Featured Designer Emilio Pucci

Silhouette Short, fitted

Detail Vibrant swirling print

History André Courrèges, Christian Dior, Norman Norell

Famous Betty Grable, Lauren Bacall

shorts

worn by Kelli, decorator

Before 1920 the only person one was likely to see wearing a pair of short pants was male—and under the age of twelve. But by the '20s the term "shorts" was coming into general usage and women were finding them useful wear for sports like tennis and cycling. The '30s were the golden age of resort wear and the couturier Mainbocher showed them for the beach, while in the '40s shorter, decidedly sexy versions turned up on barracks walls, sported by the likes of Lauren Bacall and Betty Grable. When the boys came home, shorts took on a more sedate, suburban persona, and were worn mostly by housewives for backyard entertaining. Although widely accepted, they were not considered street wear and so were still exempt from the dictates of fashion.

As it did so many other things, the '60s changed all of that. Everybody from André Courrèges to Christian Dior was suddenly showing shorts outfits in styles that mirrored the "youthquake" dresses and trousers of the era. Supermodel Twiggy posed in short black shorts and a matching waistcoat. Girls wore "baby doll" shorts with puff sleeved blouses, or short jumpsuits with "space-age" overtones. With hemlines hovering up to a foot above the knee, shorts were just another choice, but when in the late '60s designers decided to lower the boom with the maxi skirt, shorts were suddenly the only game in town. "Hot pants"—very short shorts in formal materials—were first introduced in Europe in 1970, and by 1971 Americans were wearing them

"The two lengths echo the fashion of the late '60s when maxi coats were worn atop micromini skirts."

60s

Silhouette Straight
Detail Matching studded belt
History Rebels without a cause, cowboys
Famous Bianca Jagger

the boot-cut pant

The British earnestly explain that the fashion for boots (and "boot-cut" pants with a hem wide enough to accommodate them) came about in the late '50s after women noticed the chic footwear of the Royal Air Force. Americans say it was all the fault of James Dean. Dean, Marlon Brando, and the other motorcycle-riding hunks of that era wore tight pants (of course) but with hems cut wide to accommodate the big black boots their mode of transportation required. They were not the first to make this sartorial accommodation: The cowboy—another American icon who lived and died with his boots on—had already discovered the practicality of this roomy silhouette.

The cowboy's lady wouldn't have considered wearing any pants at all and when her grand-daughter finally got around to it—in the '30s and '40s—the prevailing fashion was plenty wide enough for the pumps and sandals with which they were worn. But by the late '50s the slim cigarette pant was in—and so were boots—and those who tried to wear them together found it a very tight fit indeed. Boots were even more popular in the early '60s and designers continued to cut their pants wide enough to assure a neat, comfortable fit. Bell-bottoms, which appeared in the mid-'60s were an extreme manifestation of this trend, but

worn by Deborah, event planner

70s

Eva's white shirt is a man's button-down version that once belonged to her father. Walking the dog on a Sunday she rolls up her sleeves and goes monochromatic with a pair of tight white jeans. She's a chic blank canvas ready for whimsical touches like a '60s "leopard" felt hat that she found at a Florida thrift shop and a pair of red shoes. At work her white shirt is all business. Paired with a graphic black-and-white giraffe-skin straight skirt from the '60s, it projects a confident look, simple and straightforward—yet sexy in its subtlety, especially when she adds black high-heeled mules. A white shirt with early '70s silver lamé bell-bottoms for evening? Why not? Confidently combining the ultimate classic and the ultimate trend item, Eva tucks in her shirt at the waist and rolls up her sleeves. It looks fabulous. Personal style has its rewards.

Featured Designer Norma Kamali

Silhouette Wraps the body

Detail Scalloped edges

History Madeleine Vionnet, Claire McCardell, Halston, Diane Von Furstenberg

Famous Halstonettes

the wrap

worn by Hayley, artist

dress

Fashions at the turn of the 20th century were nothing if not complicated. There was method to the madness. The more buttons, fastenings, and layers an outfit possessed, the more obvious it was that the wearer was a real lady, with a personal maid to help her dress. Then came World War I. The era that followed was determinedly modern and democratic, and women wanted to look and feel the part. Designers began to make clothes with simple, wrap fronts that proclaimed their independence from servants and the old ways. It turned out to be an inherently elegant look, and by the '30s it was being used by Lanvin and Vionnet in glamorous evening dresses with

bodices that wrapped and tied to show the figure underneath. Schiaparelli's sari evening dresses of that decade were based on traditional Indian dress, the original wrap silhouette.

The wrap front was a favorite of American sportswear designers Claire McCardell, Elizabeth Hawes and Bonnie Cashin who, throughout the '30s, '40s, and '50s, created an entire genre of clothing based on stretched, wrapped, and tied fabric. They made all-American, democratic clothes: a couple of easy movements and you were ready to go in a dress that took its shape from you, not vice versa. This now-classic look reappeared in

70s

90s

90s

"more limo than motorcycle"

Bethann snaps it open to almost to the hip, to show purple crochet bell-bottoms underneath. The pants are more fun than stockings and are another surprisingly classic look—one used by designers like Jean-Paul Gaultier and Comme des Garçons in the '90s. A gray cashmere double-breasted jacket coordinates with the knit pants and pulls everything together. In a professional setting the skirt works better closed to the knee. The black leather jacket from the same era is more limo than motorcycle and looks crisp with a white shirt, open from the bottom up, like the skirt. For evening, Bethann gets out an ethnic shawl from her large collection and fashions herself an evening blouse. With suede, patterns, and layers she's created an outfit reminiscent of Saint Laurent's "rich peasant" look of 1976—another classic.

Featured Designer Ossie Clark
Silhouette On the bias
Detail Hand-painted silk
History Madeleine Vionnet,
Gabrielle Chanel, Elsa Schiaparelli
Famous Bianca Jagger

bias-cut dress

worn by Milly, decorator

The bias-cut dress is a bit of a mystery. How does the simple act of cutting fabric on the diagonal produce such a sinuous, clingy, graceful line? One who certainly knew the answer was the '20s Parisian designer Madeleine Vionnet—the inventor of this revolutionary cut. Her clothes stunned their stylish audience and changed fashion history. For the first time a dress was cut to follow the lines of the body, revealing its curves. Suddenly clothes were all about shape, not applied decoration. Throughout the '20s and '30s, designers like Gabrielle Chanel and Elsa Schiaparelli made the bias cut their own, creating the slinky satin gowns that have come to symbolize that glamorous era. Along the way they also produced a series of bias-cut dresses with uneven "handkerchief" hems, tiered skirts, and sleeves like butterfly wings. Adding to the modernity of the look was Schiaparelli's penchant for commissioning fabric by contemporary artists like Jean Cocteau and Christian Bérard.

In the late '60s it was déjà vu all over again. It was the era of the "rich hippie" and the "gypsy"—the romantic, ethnic looks popularized by Saint Laurent and others. Dresses were again sporting multiple layers, winged sleeves, uneven hems, and drifting scarves in printed gauzy fabrics. Among the best of the offerings for evening were the bias-cut extravaganzas by designer Ossie Clark, the fashion wunderkind of "swinging London." This early '70s example has the signature body-conscious shape that made Clark famous. Its many bias-cut layers somehow manage to conceal and reveal the body at the same time. Like many of Clark's best efforts, it is made of a silk chiffon hand-painted by Clark's wife, Celia Birtwell.

70s

80s

This dress still looks as marvelous on Milly as it did the day she bought it. It's also wonderfully versatile. Its sheerness, comfortable fit, and wrinkle-proof fabric make it a surprisingly useful beach cover-up. Here Milly wears it over a vintage Pucci bikini—mixing patterns so disparate they don't fight each other. Equipped with a straw bag bought from a street vendor, sandals, and sunglasses, she is ready to hit the sands. Back at work, the same dress makes a good first layer for a businesslike '80s navy wool blazer from Ralph Lauren. The jacket's length smooths her skirt layers into a sleeker line and black fabric boots add another daytime touch. Her coordinating Roberta di Camerino portfolio from the same era as the dress is another great find. To segue from office to evening event, she has only to lose the blazer and slip into a pair of silk shoes (and a sheer bodysuit, if she's feeling modest) and let Ossie Clark do his magic.

"It was the era of the 'rich hippie'
and the 'gypsy.'"

Silhouette cropped
Detail Feathers instead of fur
History Bullfighters, Yves Saint Laurent, Geoffrey Beene
Famous Cher

the bolero

worn by "Dabber" (Alexandra), actress

In the late 19th century some enterprising style maker noticed how attractive Spanish bullfighters looked in their distinctive cropped jackets. It was the beginning of the silhouette known as the "bolero"—a fashion classic that has endured for over one hundred years. Popular at the turn of the century, the bolero was briefly eclipsed by the more military "safari" look during World War I but returned in force in the '30s when its sleek, unfussy lines (devoid of any collar or fastenings) enhanced but did not obscure the sinuous, flowing dresses that characterized that decade.

In the '40s the bolero took on a whole other life in the guise of the "chubby"—a waist-length jacket made of long-haired fur, with wide straight arms and no collar. This distinctive outerwear was the succès fou of that "boogie-woogie" decade. In Patrick Dennis's classic memoir *Auntie Mame*, the hero, who is carrying on with an ambitious waitress named Bubbles, remembers that he "had to hock my studs and cuff links to pay for the bulky white fox jacket she insisted on buying. 'But honey, I gotta have a chubby!'" Saint Laurent reprised this evocative silhouette in his '40s-inspired collection of 1970 and again in 1979–1980, sparking a general revival of interest in the chubby and elevating it to the status of fashion classic within the already timeless genre of the bolero.

40s

113.

70s

70s

This black and white ostrich-feather number from the early '70s is an updated version of the '40s chubby. It's also pure fun. When Dabber entertains at home, she greets her guests wearing an unexpected combination—her ostrich chubby and another '70s classic, a high-waisted, halter-neck cotton jumpsuit with crocheted trim. Heading out to an audition, Dabber stays warm and cuts a striking figure—fashionable but funky. Worn with a basic uniform of sneakers, jeans, and tank, her chubby seems a statement of self-confidence and sly wit. When night falls, the chubby is in its element, evoking a string of glamorous evenings stretching back to the '40s. Dabber creates instant elegance with a '80s black slip skirt, a pair of high-heeled stretch polyester satin boots, and her seriously sexy ostrich-feather bolero jacket. Another plus: Its bulk emphasizes the slim, sleek lines down below.

80s

Silhouette Pajama
Detail Embroidery
History Gabrielle Chanel, Jean Patou
Famous Caresse Crosby

pajamas 20s

worn by Neva, real estate broker

Not every fashion classic is Western in origin. Take this Chinese pajama suit—hip-length jacket, mandarin collar, fabric frog closing, straight- leg drawstring pant, all of fine embroidered silk. It was made in China in the style of a fine mandarin robe in the late '20s but its simple lines, subtle colors, and exquisite floral patterns make it a timeless addition to any wardrobe—East or West. Like any classic, its quality is no small part of its charm. Beware the synthetic fabrics, garish colors, and machine-made embroidery of many "Chinese" suits from the '40s, '50s, and beyond. They are fine for a Halloween costume.

What makes this outfit eminently wearable from decade to decade is the same combination that makes a Saint Laurent suit a classic—skilled handwork, fine silk, proportion, and elegance. Think of it as the Eastern version of couture.

This suit was made for the Western market, but its silhouette would be familiar to any Chinese woman. Two-piece outfits of this kind have been worn in the Far East since ancient times. Western women were a bit slower to appreciate the joys of the pajama (a Hindustani word from the Persian *pai*, meaning leg, and *jaman*, meaning a garment), but by the '20s they had

"For work I complete this look with a pair of loafers"

caught on nicely. In that decade designers like Chanel introduced the lounging suit and the beach pajama, designed to take wealthy holiday-makers from plage to cocktail bar. Imbued with the status of that envied group, the pajama became a fashionable wardrobe staple of the '30s. Shapes varied: The trousers might be more or less wide, the jacket might cover a bare halter top, but this traditional Eastern silhouette was the favorite of many. In fact, a savvy woman of that era might have worn this little number and wowed them at a drinks party in Nice or Palm Beach. The craze for exoticism that followed the 1922 discovery of King Tut's tomb may have added a bit to its charm, but by the '30s the beautiful, well-made, embroidered Chinese pajama had attained the status of a true fashion classic.

Like any other "separates," these two pieces are extremely versatile. Wear them together as a hostess outfit at your own casual get-together (no shoes required), or dress up the same suit with high-heeled black sandals and every fake jewel you own. Proceed to the opera. For her workday, Neva has borrowed her husband's white Oxford shirt, rolled up the pants to capri length, and completed the look with a pair of businesslike loafers. It's an easy-fit, no-fuss outfit but striking and practically seasonless as well. For the evening, throw the jacket over a slinky dress like this Stephen Burrows design from the early '70s. The blue of the jersey dress is one of the colors in the embroidery, and black sandals pull everything together. Why wear a traditional Chinese jacket over such a bare, obviously Western dress? That's just the point. Its easy cardigan shape is the perfect foil for such a body-conscious choice, and the contrast of materials and styles makes you notice both pieces more. Finally, the jacket is black, and black is almost always right.

Featured Designer Geoffrey Beene

Silhouette Trapeze

Detail Black ostrich feathers

History Gabrielle Chanel, Bonnie Cashin, Yves Saint Laurent, Calvin Klein

Famous Donna Reed, Marilyn Monroe

worn by Amy, writer

the car coat

The term "car coat" puts a suburban spin on a classic silhouette that goes back to turn-of-the-century American military dress. Long bulky coats made it difficult for sailors to slide smoothly in and out of hatches, so they were issued a "pea coat"—a nifty hip-length, navy blue double-breasted wool number with notched lapels. It was so attractive that people of both sexes have been wearing it ever since—but that is another story. By 1927, Gabrielle Chanel was showing "sports coats" of a similar fingertip length—a silhouette that continued to be popular throughout the '30s and '40s. Single or double-breasted, swing-back or straight, the shorter coat was a useful and frequent addition to a woman's wardrobe, particularly during World War II when, due to the rationing of silk stockings, pants were worn much more often.

After the war it seemed as if the entire suburban female population was spending the day in the car. Designers like Bonnie Cashin thoughtfully provided fingertip-length coats in wool, canvas, corduroy, and other durable fabrics—coats that stayed out of the driver's way as she slid in and out of the Chevy wagon. These were promptly christened "car coats." Yves Saint Laurent probably never saw a station wagon in his life, but when he reprised the pea coat in his 1962 collection, the style was eagerly adopted by American carpoolers. The fingertip-length coat lost its automotive moniker sometime in the '60s, but the silhouette continued to be used by designers, including Chester Weinberg and Perry Ellis in the '70s, Cathy Hardwick in the '80s and Calvin Klein in the '90s.

80s

"The year of a Beene design doesn't matter..."

90s

"It exists out of time like any other enduring work of art."

From the closet of Amy, one of America's leading vintage collectors, this version is about as fabulous as a car coat can get. It's from Geoffrey Beene's 1988 collection—intricately quilted silk tartan with gold thread, embellished with black ostrich feathers—the perfect example of Beene's penchant for juxtaposing unusual fabrics and for blurring the distinction between day and night. Great things like this can turn up almost anywhere: Just after purchasing her coat Amy saw another example in a thrift shop that was mislabeled "Dolce & Gabbana" and selling for a fraction of its original cost. "I called a friend and told her to rush over," she recalls. "I would happily have owned two, but I decided not to be greedy." By day Amy wears her unforgettable coat over a 1997 Beene jumpsuit in black wool jersey. By night she pulls out all the stops, wearing it over a lipstick-red pleated chiffon Geoffrey Beene dress from 1998. "The year of a Beene design doesn't matter," says Amy, who wears his work exclusively. "It exists out of time like any other enduring work of art."

Featured Designer Christian Dior
Silhouette Trapeze
Detail No closure apparatus
History Gabrielle Chanel, Jean Muir, Geoffrey Beene, Cristóbal Balenciaga
Famous Audrey Hepburn

50s the swing coat

worn by Ghislaine, business consultant

The inconveniences of "motoring" at the turn of the century had a surprisingly lasting effect on fashion. The open cars and rutted dirt roads of that era produced so much dust that women passengers were obliged to wear "dusters"—long, loose, unfitted coats in linen or wool—to protect their clothes. Since ladies who had never been near a car wanted to look as if they went driving every day, designers provided outerwear with the loose, fashionable silhouette their clients craved. As cars became a practical fact of life the duster lost its magic and gradually evolved into the swing coat—a more controlled, tailored version, swinging from the shoulders to a flaring hem. Throughout the '20s, '30s, and early '40s designers like Chanel and Vionnet created sports coats and long suit jackets in this jaunty shape, ceasing only when the war and restrictions on fabric use mandated a slimmer look.

As soon as the war ended the swing coat was back—with a vengeance. Tentlike coats of all descriptions were the silhouette of the '50s—an attractive contrast to the slim, structured clothes of that era and a perfect complement to the wider triangular dresses that were also being produced. The '50s ended but the swing coat never really went away—enduring through all of the following decades, done by almost every designer at one time or another, including Jean Muir, Geoffrey Beene, and Christian Dior.

This beauty might have been picked up yesterday, but its lucky owner is glad it's almost forty years old. It was made by Christian Dior in the '50s, in an era when nothing from that house could be bought off the rack, from one piece of fine khaki-colored silk. It's like a fine piece of machinery—cut on the bias, seamless—perfectly shaped and with no buttons to mar its lines. It's also unbelievably versatile and wearable through three seasons, over almost anything. A bikini? Why not? All-American khaki frames Ghislaine's bathing suit in its all-American colors. It's a nice change when classics can have some shock value. For work—no shocks. Ghislaine wears a riding jacket from the late '40s, a white shirt borrowed from her boyfriend, and modern black corduroy trousers. The coat is not only a perfect finish for this ensemble but also slides on easily over the jacket. At night, the coat's silky finish and classic lines come to the fore again. Ghislaine uses it as a tunic over a long '60s Pucci skirt worn with ballet flats—another '50s look that works just fine here.

Silhouette Form-fitting
Detail Lace trim
History The boudoir
Famous Elizabeth Taylor

the slip
worn by Madley,
photographer's
assistant

30s

The undergarment called a "slip" has been around since the early 19th century, but the sexy, slithery slip we know and love is a bit more recent. It first made its appearance in the '20s—a slightly fitted silk chemise, often lace trimmed, with thin shoulder straps. In that decade it was sometimes difficult to tell the difference between a slip and the street dress on top, which appeared to be modeled after it. The brief, bare tank dresses of that era were a scandal, causing preachers to complain that ladies were doing the Charleston in their underwear. By the '30s and '40s the "slip" dress had hit the Big Screen, worn by the likes of Ava Gardner and Ginger Rogers. No star would ever appear in her underwear, but these dresses were the next best thing in slinky bareness.

Times changed. Elizabeth Taylor wore a real slip as Maggie in the '50s classic film *Cat on a Hot Tin Roof* and she looked so great that she introduced a whole generation of women to the possibilities of such a garment, which had been hidden beneath the stiff, constructed dresses of the '50s. Nylon had replaced silk after World War II and anybody could afford a pretty, shapely slip—even if only Elizabeth Taylor dared to wear it outside of the boudoir. Twenty years later the slip had changed roles again. Actual underwear was now minimal but the underwear look had hit the streets. Slip dresses with spaghetti straps were big in the '70s, and Calvin Klein's slip dress in metallic lace and chiffon looks like a cross between a corset and a slip. Late '90s dresses by Dolce & Gabbana, Donna Karan, Prada, and Tom Ford are simple satin and lace versions of traditional pre-'60s slips. Fashion had once again come full circle.

Madley bought this '30s lavender-gray silk beauty in a flea market for $3. It started life as a slip, but because it's well made and of beautiful material it looks like any slip dress from the '90s. For a funky

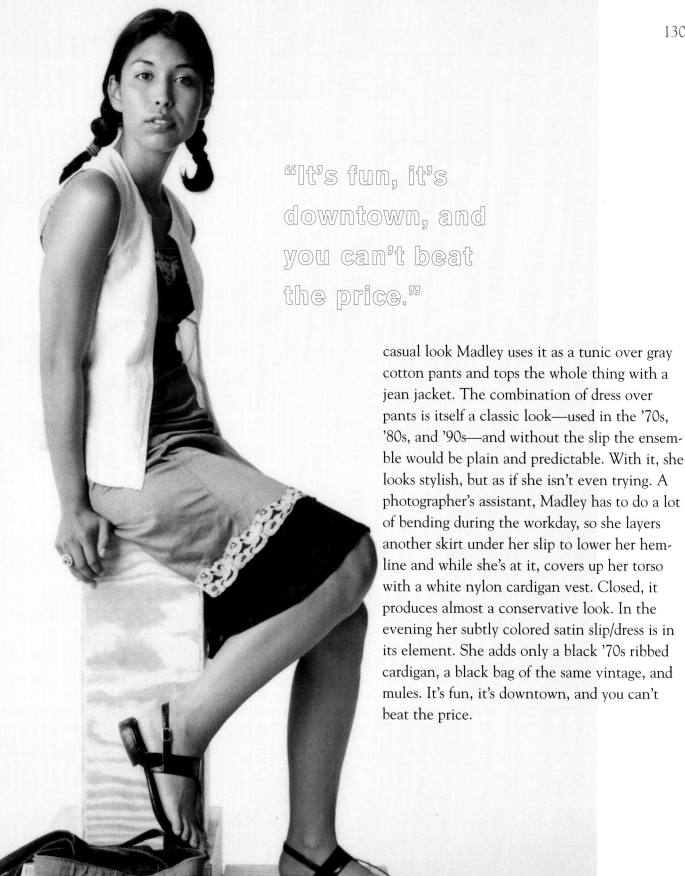

"It's fun, it's downtown, and you can't beat the price."

casual look Madley uses it as a tunic over gray cotton pants and tops the whole thing with a jean jacket. The combination of dress over pants is itself a classic look—used in the '70s, '80s, and '90s—and without the slip the ensemble would be plain and predictable. With it, she looks stylish, but as if she isn't even trying. A photographer's assistant, Madley has to do a lot of bending during the workday, so she layers another skirt under her slip to lower her hemline and while she's at it, covers up her torso with a white nylon cardigan vest. Closed, it produces almost a conservative look. In the evening her subtly colored satin slip/dress is in its element. She adds only a black '70s ribbed cardigan, a black bag of the same vintage, and mules. It's fun, it's downtown, and you can't beat the price.

70s

Featured Designer Celia Birtwell
Silhouette A-line
Detail Tomato red
History Christian Dior, Mary Quant,
André Courrèges, Pierre Cardin,
Emanuel Ungaro
Famous Jackie O

Midcentury Americans were nuts about the triangle. Stylish young couples entertained in "A-frame" houses and, on the fashion scene, couturier Christian Dior launched his "A-line," showing dresses with a distinctive triangular silhouette, which widened from small shoulders to a broad pleated or stiffened hem. When Yves Saint Laurent took over for Monsieur Dior in 1958, his "trapeze line" of that year was yet another triangular silhouette—less stiff, but still rather extreme with its tentlike flaring lines. It was left to Mary Quant (the about-to-be-famous designer of Swinging London) to introduce the gently body-skimming A-line dress that was to become her trademark and that would put the A-line silhouette permanently on the fashion map.

A-line dress
worn by Carrie, graduate student

60s

It was a shape that dominated the '60s, used by Quant, Courrèges, Cardin, Ungaro, Anne Klein, and others in a decade's worth of short, flaring dresses, skirts, and coats. The silhouette put no emphasis on the breasts, waist, or hips and so was inherently young—the watchword of the '60s. It was also sleek and aerodynamic like the spacecraft that inspired so many of the designs of the era. Best of all it was slimming, comfortable, and extremely easy to wear—a fashion solution so obvious that everybody wondered why they hadn't thought of it sooner. Needless to say, the A-line silhouette continued to be used by designers during the '70s, was briefly eclipsed by the "power clothes" of the '80s, only to reappear in the early '90s.

This dynamite '60s example in a tomato red wool knit is from Celia Birtwell, the influential fabric and fashion designer and wife of fellow Mod London designer Ossie Clark. Its length makes it the perfect tunic, here worn for a casual weekend event, cinched with a purple cashmere scarf (yes, purple and red, try it) tied as an obi and topping gray wool three-quarter length "pirate pants" from the '50s. Carrie's shoes are vintage too—Christian Dior from the '60s. Once she had the dress, Carrie couldn't resist this beautifully tailored, navy suede Ungaro coat from the early '70s, in the same A-line shape, piped in the same red. The pair are the perfect workday ensemble (especially when accessorized with '50s sunglasses designed by Venice art collector/jet-setter Peggy Guggenheim). In the evening, Carrie pulls on her low-heeled, snakeskin-patterned, gray "pleather" go-go boots and adds a '70s suede and feather necklace she found in a Palm Beach junk shop for $5. Her '20s hair (à la Louise Brooks), '60s dress, and '70s necklace add up to a timeless look—the only kind she's interested in.

70s

60s

Featured Designer Yves Saint Laurent

Silhouette Line

Detail Straight

History Gabrielle Chanel, Claire McCardell

Famous Marian McEvoy

the
worn by Marian, editor
straight skirt

Like many of fashion's simplest innovations, the straight skirt can be traced to the pen of Gabrielle Chanel, around 1920. Before that groundbreaking designer, skirts were still held out with hoops or petticoats, were draped, or sported bustles or over-skirts. Even the simplest flared in the proper "feminine" way. Designer Paul Poiret led the way into the future by taking women out of corsets and into straight tunic dresses, but it was Gabrielle Chanel who first made suits featuring the slim, simple, straight skirt that has become a constant, classic silhouette of the 20th century.

Its length, however, has been anything but constant. In 1923 skirts were still ankle-length, they rose to the knee in the late '20s, only to drop again during the '30s and '40s. Daytime fashions hovered between knee and midcalf, while evening looks swept the floor. Every new season designers called the shots, declaring last year's length passé, sending women scurrying to their dressmakers for alterations or new, more fashionable clothes. This scenario reached a crescendo in the late '60s when, tiring of the miniskirt, designers suddenly lowered hems by several feet—declaring the return of the "maxi." This time not everybody obeyed, and minis and maxis were seen side by side on fashionable women. This skirt's distinctive front-button styling dates to the '40s and the American pioneers Claire McCardell and Bonnie Cashin. Nobody, these designers seemed to be saying, has a personal maid to "do" her up the back anymore. Buttons were proudly accessible—celebrated as useful tools—as in Claire McCardell's skirt of 1944, with its buttons straight down the front all the way to the ground.

"The straight skirt can be traced to the pen of Gabrielle Chanel, around 1920."

80s

50s

Marian's wool crepe example was made by Yves Saint Laurent in the '80s, but it could have been made in any decade since the '40s. It can take you anywhere. For a weekend look, lighten up with a '50s cotton striped "sailor" shirt and a few ropes of faux pearls. To go a notch dressier, Marian tops the skirt with another '50s find, a man's long black linen tuxedo-style jacket with velvet trim. Add vintage gloves ($5 in a thrift shop) and she's ready to turn heads at an editorial meeting. The same skirt works just as well in the evening, topped with a black bodysuit, a silk sari stole, and lots of Indian jewelry.

Featured Designer André Courrèges
Silhouette Straight
Detail Patent leather shoulder straps
History Christian Dior, Hubert de Givenchy
Famous Babe Paley

the shift dress

60s

worn by Shyama,
magazine columnist

60s

The "sack," the "chemise," the "shift," the "sheath"—by any name, we're talking about the straight, flattering, waistless silhouette that began life in the late '50s. Before that date women had contorted their bodies into S-shaped curves, flattened those curves into boyish, dropped-waist tank dresses, and worn all kinds of other unforgiving silhouettes from the bias cut to the "New Look." Then, in 1957, Christian Dior introduced "The Free Line" and Hubert de Givenchy brought out "The Sack" and every other designer from Bonnie Cashin to Emilio Pucci got on the bandwagon. The result was an elegant, rather architectural shape that had less to do with breasts and hips and more to do with the clean streamlines of the 20th century.

Women loved it—but predictably, their menfolk did not. The solution was to taper those original, loose, sexless silhouettes until they just skimmed the figure. Everyone was happy and the shift became the classic dress shape of the late 20th century. It didn't hurt that First Lady Jackie Kennedy, the biggest fashion icon of her day, wore almost nothing but shifts or two-piece shift ensembles. Jackie favored solid, sherbetlike colors and little adornment, but over the years the shift has lent itself to everything from Yves Saint Laurent's Mondrianesque geometry to Pucci's distinctive patterns. It's been with us in every decade—used more recently by the likes of Gianni Versace, Dolce & Gabbana, Giorgio Armani, and Azzedine Alaia—and will no doubt be with us for many more.

If you closed your eyes and pictured the classic "little black dress" you'd probably come up with something very much like this. In what decade was it made? What difference does it make? This example, a Courrèges off-the-rack dress from the '60s, is beautifully made in a soft wool with a lot

5Os

"In what decade was it made?"

of body and features a charming pair of patent leather shoulder straps with decorative bows; it was bought at a vintage clothing show for a very reasonable $300. For evening it's perfect on its own; Shyama needs only a '20s beaded bag and a pair of contemporary strappy sandals to look right for almost any occasion. During daylight hours the dress recedes and becomes the ideal background for almost any look—like this cool, funky one—created with the addition of a '50s faux leopard bolero and bag. On the weekend the dress recedes even further, acting as a handy black wool skirt to wear with a '60s ribbed cashmere turtleneck sweater in cheerful apple green. When night falls, whip off your sweater and start all over again.

90s

Featured Designer Emilio Pucci
Silhouette Cropped
Detail Pink fringe
History Elsa Schiaparelli, Gabrielle Chanel
Famous Annette Funicello

"The cropped pant is such a classic."

pedal
60s pushers

worn by Beth, store owner

Elsa Schiaparelli and Gabrielle Chanel wouldn't have dreamed of calling three-quarter-length trousers "clam diggers" or "high-water pants." But during the '30s each of these rival designers came up with this flattering, youthful silhouette and used it in collections of elegant beach and resort wear. It was not until the '40s that the three-quarter pant earned the first of its many nicknames. Bicycles were being used to deal with wartime gas shortages and because shorter pants didn't get caught in the spokes, they became extremely popular. Somebody decided to call them "pedal pushers" and the name stuck.

In the '50s the three-quarter-length silhouette picked up a few other labels as well. Emilio Pucci called his version "pirate pants"—probably a reference to his beloved Mediterranean Sea—and used them in his resort collections throughout the late '40s, '50s, and early '60s. Soon the length was part of the international Jet Set uniform as well as a favorite of that other '50s style-setting group—

American teenagers. Their favorite look featured bobby socks, ponytails, and denim pedal pushers. Like its tighter, side-slit sister the capri pant, pedal pushers were also adopted by the '50s "beat generation," who wore them with black turtlenecks and flat shoes. Suburbanites of the '60s also liked the shorter pant, which they rechristened "clam diggers." The silhouette made sporadic appearances in the '70s and '80s, and in the '90s returned to prominence as the cropped pant in the collections of designers like Marc Jacobs.

"The cropped pant is such a classic," says Beth, the co-owner of a hip downtown New York clothing store. "I love this pair because it's totally modern—the way vintage clothes should look." On a Saturday afternoon Beth wears her fringed, pink silk jersey pants, made by Pucci in the early '60s, with a tie-dye, tank top, jean jacket and flip-flops. "The pants are a little fancy-schmancy but the tie-dye dresses them right down."

155.

"I love this pair...it's totally **modern, the way** vintage clothes should look."

On a workday Beth replaces the tank with a Bonnie Cashin wool poncho, also from the '60s, in an unusual combination of pink and caramel, and slides on an armful of Indian bracelets and a pair of Moroccan pony-fur slippers. "This look is what I'd call 'casual chic,'" says Beth. "I feel totally dressed but totally comfortable." In the evening a black and white color scheme unleashes the inherent elegance of the pants. Beth pairs them with a cashmere racer-back tank and a cashmere and silk shawl and steps into black silk heels with rhinestone buckles. She's ready for dinner at a restaurant—or New Year's Eve—and nobody there will look more attractive and original than she.

Featured Designer Bonnie Cashin, Jacques Fath
Silhouette Wraps the body
Detail Black rayon jersey
History Madeleine Vionnet, Adrian, Hattie Carnegie, Claire McCardell, Yves Saint Laurent
Famous Jean Harlow, Greta Garbo

the halter top
worn by Lisa, TV executive

By the time this halter top was made, ca. 1975, it was already a classic. Its simple construction makes it unavoidably sexy—clinging lightly to the neck, dividing and draping across the breasts—while leaving arms, shoulders, and back quite bare. Not surprisingly, the halter made its first appearance in the '30s when it was used frequently by designers of the body-conscious, glamorous gowns that characterized that slinky decade. In 1937, Parisienne Madeleine Vionnet paired a halter top with a shower of pleats in gold lamé, while American designers like Adrian and Hattie Carnegie dressed Hollywood beauties like Jean Harlow and Greta Garbo in halter-neck gowns of seductive satin and silk chiffon.

The '50s saw the form reborn under the talented fingers of American sportswear designers Claire McCardell and Bonnie Cashin. Simplicity and ease—not sexiness—was their goal, although in the end they achieved both. Their clothes are ingeniously constructed so that they wrap the body, allowing the wearer to form the garment's final shape. Eschewing the darts and other fussy requirements of many '50s clothes, these designers favored the halter bodice because it was a simple drape of fabric that emphasized what was already there. By the time the silhouette was reprised by Saint Laurent and others in the '70s, the halter had joined the ranks of fashion classics.

70s

This example was made in black rayon jersey in the '70s–about the time Yves Saint Laurent was showing what he called "tight wrap bodices," with wide-bottom trousers, much like these. Lisa's casual look works just as well today, balancing the eye-catching, psychedelic pattern of her '70s knit bell-bottom trousers with a solid black bodice in a similar stretch fabric. Its sleek, tight form is an excellent counterpoint to their ample folds.

60s

20s

40s

When she wears the same piece to work, Lisa covers it with a Bonnie Cashin all-weather coat from the '60s—as easy as an overshirt—in a timeless taupe and white check. The prescient Cashin herself might have paired these two sculptural, unfussy shapes. A contemporary white knee-length skirt and a black handbag pulls everything together.

The same halter takes on a completely different look when worn with a full-length cranberry satin ball skirt made by Jacques Fath in the early '40s. (Fath was known to combat the sadness of wartime Paris with beautiful colors like this.) In its evening guise, the halter is elegant—almost Grecian—an example of classical draping, as it shows off Lisa's shapely shoulders and arms. It's sexy too. Paired with such a gleaming, flowing skirt, even a jersey top can evoke every satin gown Jean Harlow ever wore. Lisa has also upped the ante with a little heat from sunny Spain. Taking advantage of her outfit's flamencoesque black and red color scheme, she's thrown a '20s black beaded shawl over her shoulders. *Olé!*

Silhouette Unstructured
Detail Embroidery, frogging, braid
History Traditional ethnic design
Famous Yves Saint Laurent

"Timeless" the moroccan jacket

worn by Hamish, editor

"Timeless" is how Hamish, a magazine editor and collector of vintage clothes, describes the chocolate brown Moroccan jacket he bought several years ago in Marrakech. "An elderly man there made them for many years," he explains. "Yves Saint Laurent, Fernando Sanchez, and many others wore them. Now someone else is making them, carrying on the tradition, and the look never changes." Hamish's example is made of a heavy wool felt, embellished with embroidery, black braiding, and frogging. It's an ethnic look but it's also very Middle European—rather like a Crimean War uniform.

"A Moroccan jacket is quite formal in its decoration, but it's made like an unstructured cardigan, so one can easily dress it up or down." Wearing a pair of tobacco-colored Brooks Brothers trousers, a lavender shirt, and going sockless in suede loafers, Hamish completes a casual but very individual weekend look by topping it with his Moroccan

jacket. The shape is so modern and unobtrusive that at first glance one wonders where all the magic is coming from—until the eye registers the subtle braid, embroidery, and heavy, unusual fabric.

On assignment for the magazine, Hamish wears the same jacket with severely tapered trousers and a vest—part of a vintage tartan suit he bought at auction at Sotheby's in London. "It was made in the '50s for the fashion designer Bunny Roger, the last of the English dandies and the first to revive Edwardian clothes for men," he explains. "The mustard and mauve pattern is my favorite tartan and the buttons are 19th century, decorated with rabbits." The wider, unstructured silhouette of the Moroccan jacket is a flattering counterpoint to the tight vest and slim trousers, and its traditional ethnic design serves as an unexpected foil for the bold tartan. Each makes you more aware of the other.

The Moroccan jacket is just as successful as a dinner jacket. Worn with a classic evening shirt, black tie, and formal trousers, the jacket's decorative frogging, braid, and embroidery are as dressy as they want to be. Instead of an opera cape, Hamish wears a vintage Venetian cloth djellaba, purchased in a shop in Tangier. The silky finish of the deep yellow coat adds another note of formality while slippers made from Turkish carpet add a little exoticism and fun. The entire look—a dexterous blend of timeless Eastern and Western elements—is too classic to be costumey. "I love to incorporate vintage elements into the clothes I wear," says Hamish. "I love the sense of complete uniqueness they provide."

50s

"I love to incorporate vintage elements into the clothes I wear . . . I love the sense of complete uniqueness they provide."

Index to the clothes

coats

car coat   page 121

swing coat   page 124

double   page 77
breasted coat

suits

skirt/jacket   page 48

dress/Jacket   page 52

jumpsuit   page 41

pajamas   page 117

jackets

bolero jacket   page 113

waist-length   page 17
jacket

long double   page 57
breasted blazer

moroccan   page 152
jacket

sweaters

sweater set   page 44

turtleneck   page 21
sweater

Classics

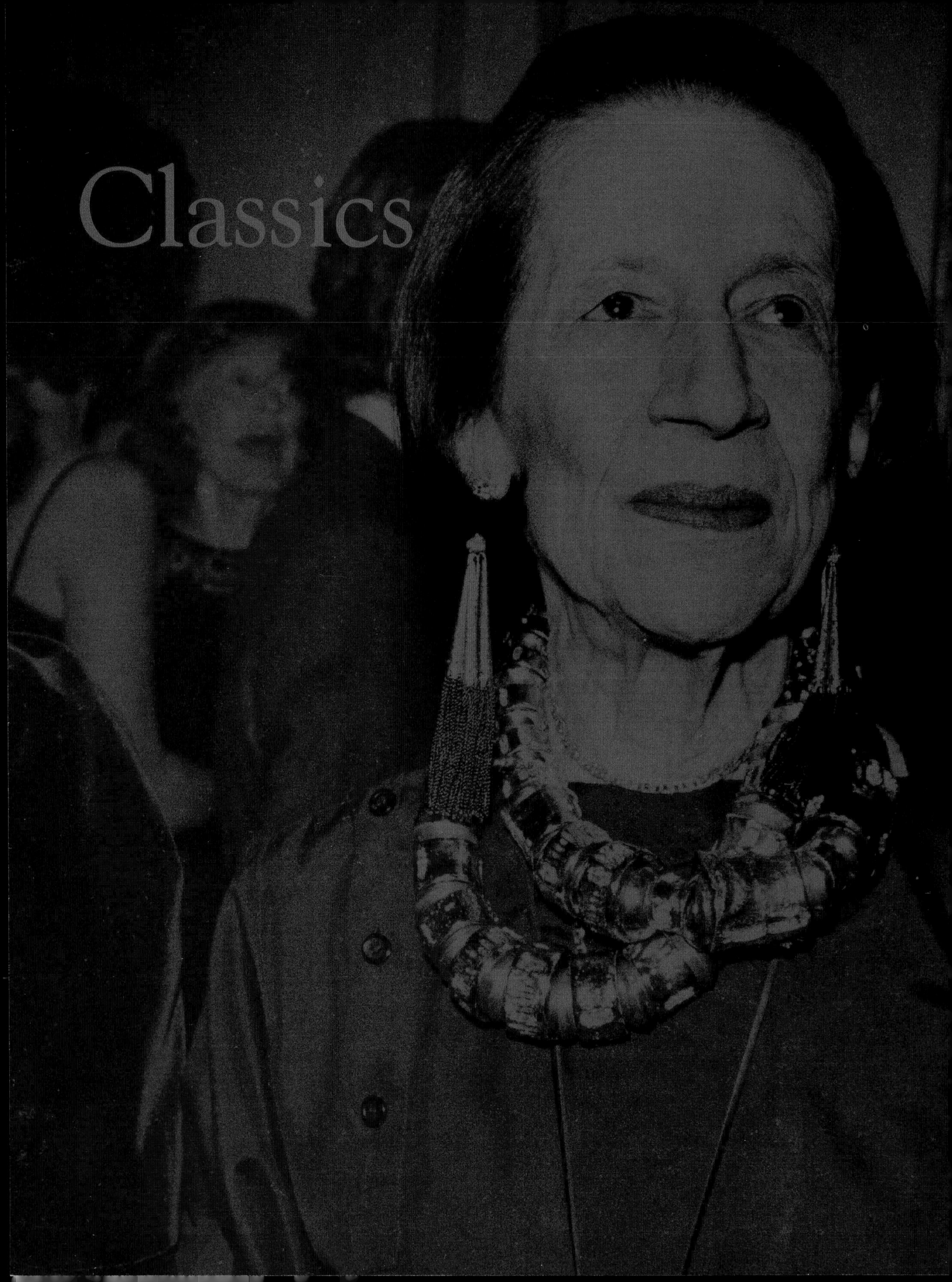

All of the clothes in this book are true classics, but these take that concept to a whole new level. Each item listed here is so easy to wear, so consistently appropriate, so eternal in its material, design, or both that, if you are lucky enough to come across an attractive vintage example, don't hesitate. You can't lose.

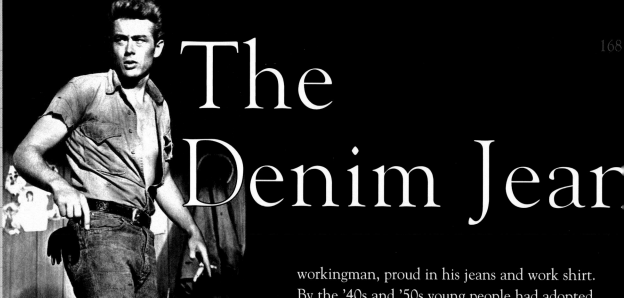

The Denim Jean

The fabric is called "denim" from the French "de Nîmes," a town in the South of France where the blue (from indigo dye) cloth originally was woven and worn, but nobody paid much attention until the 1850s, when a young entrepreneur Levi Strauss, came to California to cash in on the Gold Rush. He had thought to supply the miners with tents, but when one would-be customer tells him "you should have brought pants," Strauss changes his strategy. Soon miners are coming around looking for those "pants of Levi's," which he makes out of denim and calls "jeans" after Genoa, Italy, whose sailors were some of the first to wear denim pants.

Fast-forward one hundred and forty years. Fashion designer Bill Blass writes in *The New Yorker*: "Nothing any fashion designer has ever done has come close to having the influence of blue jeans. That Levi Strauss invention—one of the sexiest items a man or woman can wear—is the most significant contribution America has made to fashion." How did we get here, and why? Many reasons: First, there was the cowboy, that blue jean–wearing American icon with whom anybody would like to identify. Then there was the

workingman, proud in his jeans and work shirt. By the '40s and '50s young people had adopted jeans as the uniform of gentle rebellion against their elders—a rebellion that intensified to the fever pitch of the '60s when jeans came to epitomize youth and freedom for a whole generation. But by the '70s the rebellion was over; their elders were in jeans too—the designer jeans that embodied that decade. It was the era of the "lifestyle." Everyone was now "free" to wear whatever he or she liked, and what everyone liked, overwhelmingly, was jeans.

Because Bill Blass was on to something. Jeans are sexy. No matter how far away we get from the era of the cowboy, jeans are still uncontrived, unselfconscious, telegraphing the fact that we aren't trying to look good—we just do. The jean cut and stitching emphasize the figure, the soft denim clings without appearing to do so. You can wear them in any style that suits you—hip-hugger, rolled up to capri length, tight, baggy, you name it. If you go vintage you can find fabulous embroidered examples from the '60s (saves a lot of time with the needle) and other styles already nicely broken in for you. Those '70s designer numbers are also a possibility—a great fit for many women. And don't forget: There is almost nothing—from a feather boa to a Shetland sweater—that you cannot wear with jeans.

The White Shirt

Like so many fashion perennials, the white shirt was first a classic in the realm of menswear—and it all started with the Prince of Wales. Whatever the elegant, handsome prince (later the Duke of Windsor) wore was widely copied, so in the '20s when he began to appear regularly in tailored white cotton shirts with soft turn-down collars, everybody else followed suit. Gone were the stiff, high, detachable collars of the previous decades. The modern white collar shirt had been born. It was an upscale look ("white collar" vs. "blue collar") associated with royalty or at least with the kind of man who could afford a fresh clean shirt every day (not just a clean collar). It went with a business suit—not overalls.

In the '50s a more youthful but equally upscale version made its appearance. This was the "button-down" collar shirt, often made in heavier broadcloth, sported by Princeton men and Ivy League wannabes alike. By now women had also gotten into the act, wearing their boyfriends' oversized shirt with pedal pusher jeans and saddle shoes, but the white shirt was still not part of the female fashion mainstream. Although androgynous trendsetters like Marlene Dietrich and

Katharine Hepburn looked wonderful in crisp white shirts, most women were still wearing softer, more decorative blouses for street wear. By the '70s however, we had all wised up. The white shirt became a staple of everyone's wardrobe, equally at home with the preppy vests and sweaters designed by Ralph Lauren and Perry Ellis and the sleek pantsuits of Calvin Klein. In the pared-down '90s the shirt itself took center stage—worn with equally spare skirts or pants.

By then, the white shirt had come to symbolize simplicity and effortless style. It says "this is a woman who doesn't have to try—she just looks good." It shows her off—not the other way around. It's also versatile, becoming sportier or more formal, with sleeves up or down, collar open or closed. It's a neutral that's the starting point for an endless number of great outfits. Because of its very simplicity, a white shirt must be chosen carefully. Don't buy the first one you see. Look for the very best-quality cotton, the best tailoring, the most flattering silhouette. It doesn't matter if it was made originally for a woman or a man. When you've found it, remember: A perfectly tailored white shirt loses its power if worn with fussy, frilly, overpowering clothes.

Khakis

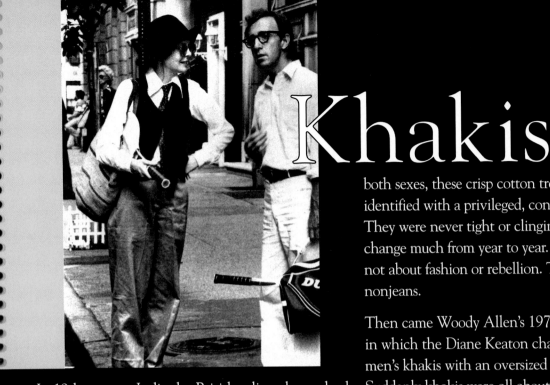

both sexes, these crisp cotton trousers were still identified with a privileged, conservative way of life. They were never tight or clinging. They didn't change much from year to year. They were certainly not about fashion or rebellion. They were the nonjeans.

Then came Woody Allen's 1977 movie *Annie Hall* in which the Diane Keaton character wore baggy men's khakis with an oversized vest and man's tie. Suddenly khakis were all about fashion—part of an idiosyncratic street look that turned old ideas upside down. After that, these classic trousers were seen as what they indeed are: versatile, neutral, well-fitting pants that go with everything. In the '80s this realization made the nationwide trend-making Gap store push khakis for people of all ages, in every income bracket. Khakis became the jeans of the late 20th century.

In 19th-century India the British ruling classes dyed their white uniforms with coffee and curry powder to combat the dust that blew constantly around them. They called the result "khaki," an Indian word for the color of dust. Khaki, now defined as a durable tan cotton twill, became the accepted tropical uniform of the British army and the American army as well. Because a lot of it was made in China, where it was purchased by the U.S. Army for uniforms for their troops in the Philippines, it also became known as "chino."

Sometime in the early 20th century men started wearing straight-legged pants made out of this same dust-resistant, practical, lightweight fabric. Not surprisingly, they became known as "khakis" or "chinos." The civilian equivalent of British officers' garb, they carried the same upper class imprimatur and sense of belonging. They became a uniform in their own right—the appropriate wear for casual occasions of all kinds—adopted by college boys and young executives on the weekends, or by anybody who wanted to look like part of those groups. Women came late to the party, wearing khakis first in the '40s and sparingly throughout the '50s and '60s. For

We can't do without them. Nobody can. Nothing is as versatile, as basic, as classic as a pair of khakis. You could go to the Gap and get a pair that's just like everybody else's, or you could shop vintage and get a pair from the '50s or '60s or '70s that are better made and just a little bit different from every other one out there. Try on men's and women's, fly front or side closure, pleated or flat front, cuffed or not, and see what suits you. Wear your pick with a huge cherry red cashmere turtleneck, thick white socks and penny loafers, or pair them with a slinky wheat-colored T-shirt, fabulous shoes, and a black blazer (bought vintage, of course). Don't wear them with a tie unless it's Halloween and you are going as Diane Keaton.

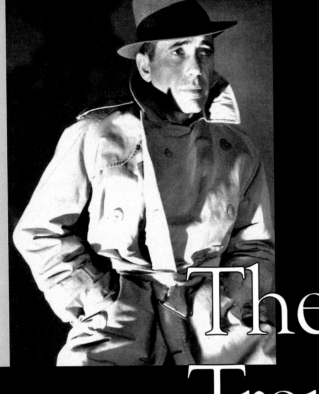

The Trench Coat

During World War I British officers were issued a new kind of outerwear designed to protect them from wind, weather, and the nasty mud of the trenches. Made of a water-repellent fabric like rubberized khaki, the coat was double-breasted with large lapels, epaulets, a fabric belt, slotted pockets, and an extra hanging yoke on the back and over the front right shoulder. All of these straps and flaps were functional and so well designed that their presence did nothing to detract from the trench coat's clean lines. The coat's close association with the British upper classes (from whose ranks most World War I officers were drawn) certainly added to its attraction, and after World War II (more British officers, more cachet) it became a popular all-purpose coat and has been worn until the present day.

Like so many other items of menswear, the trench coat was adopted by women in the practical wartime '40s. It was versatile, its neutral coloration went with everything, and in the association department it packed a double whammy: Unmistakably "appropriate" (those British officers again), it also telegraphed the subtle sexuality of a woman wearing a man's clothes. Today the trench coat remains eminently practical and versatile and although its associations are now based on photographs and film, they're still powerful: "Women may not know a lot about the history of clothes," says Valerie Steele, chief curator at Manhattan's Fashion Institute of Technology, "but they have visual memories of, say, a British officer wearing a trench coat." Not to mention the indelible image of Ingrid Bergman or Katharine Hepburn looking wonderfully sexy in a man's coat. It'll look good on you too, especially if you get a well-made example. A coat of almost any age can be a winner, as long as it's in good condition. Look for labels like "Burberry" and "Aquascutum," good sturdy khaki, purity of style, beautiful linings, and long length.

The Cashmere Sweater

First, there's the material itself—soft, warm, luxurious—named for the goats of Kashmir who live on the cold, high plateaus of Asia and produce only enough scarce underbelly wool for a single annual "harvest." This rare stuff has been at a premium for more than a century. In the mid-19th century the cashmere shawl—warm, soft, often in a subtle paisley pattern—was the most treasured part of a woman's wardrobe, costing up to a thousand 19th-century dollars. So pricey and desirable were these garments that in 1883 a young man who had jumped into the Seine to rescue a drowning woman was reported to have made a second trip to save her cashmere shawl.

The 20th-century woman preferred sweaters to shawls, but the lure of cashmere did not diminish. On its own or as part of a sweater set, the waist-length cashmere cardigan was now the object of desire. Warm but soft and light, cashmere didn't "pill" and its flat, luminous texture took color beautifully. The cashmere sweater screamed luxury and money and, by association, good taste. In the bleak cold of the wartime '40s the couturier Mainbocher even managed to make "evening sweaters" respectable. Well, they were cashmere, weren't they? In the '50s such cardigans were anointed with rich embellishments—fur, embroidery and beads—while plain sweaters were avidly collected by high school and college girls. If you didn't have at least five, you were nobody. Since then, traditional cardigans and sweater sets have continued to represent "rightness" and solid wealth, while designers like Ralph Lauren, Hanae Mori, Bill Blass, and Halston have played up their luxurious side, teaming them with taffeta or satin or concocting sweeping, floor-length versions that announce: "I can afford to have as much cashmere as I want."

You can too, if you buy vintage. If well cared for, such a sweater lasts nearly forever. Cashmere from the '40s or '50s will be thicker, softer, beautifully colored, and much more affordable than anything available today. Cardigans or sweater sets are technically the "classic" item, but anything cashmere is worth a second look. Make sure the moths have not gotten there before you.

The Leather Jacket

Talk about positive associations, the leather jacket has them coming and going. No wonder it is firmly and permanently ensconced in the realm of the classic. Known alternately as a "bomber" or "motorcycle" jacket, this simple, practical piece of outerwear is virtually a part of American history, going back eight decades. In the '20s and '30s just about the only people who wore leather jackets were pilots—dashing, adventurous men who needed warmth and didn't need long, messy coattails crumpled under them. It was still a man's world, although her devoted public was fascinated to read that Anne Morrow Lindbergh, wife of you-know-who and a pilot in her own right, wore a leather jacket when flying.

The first large group to do leather was the Army Air Corps of World War II. Warmth and practicality are even more important when you are trying to bomb cities as well as fly the plane. Both were clearly dangerous activities and when, a decade later, motorcycle-riding rebels adopted the same leather jacket it was to emphasize their own edgy lifestyle and its practical requirements. Years

later, after many viewings of *Rebel Without a Cause* (James Dean) and *The Wild One* (Marlon Brando), we tend to associate the leather jacket with positive virtues from both periods—individuality, courage, and hidden depths of sensitivity. No wonder we've seen them on every rock and roller from the '50s onward. No wonder we want one too.

By the '60s leather was everywhere and the bomber jacket entered the mainstream. Vintage examples of that era and beyond are therefore available in women's sizes while earlier examples are almost all cut for men. (They may still be an excellent fit.) For a true classic look, go for the straightforward item—black or brown, with slash pockets, a slightly blousy silhouette, and a zippered front. If it's good-quality leather, a little age will only improve things, but look out for spots and tears.

179.

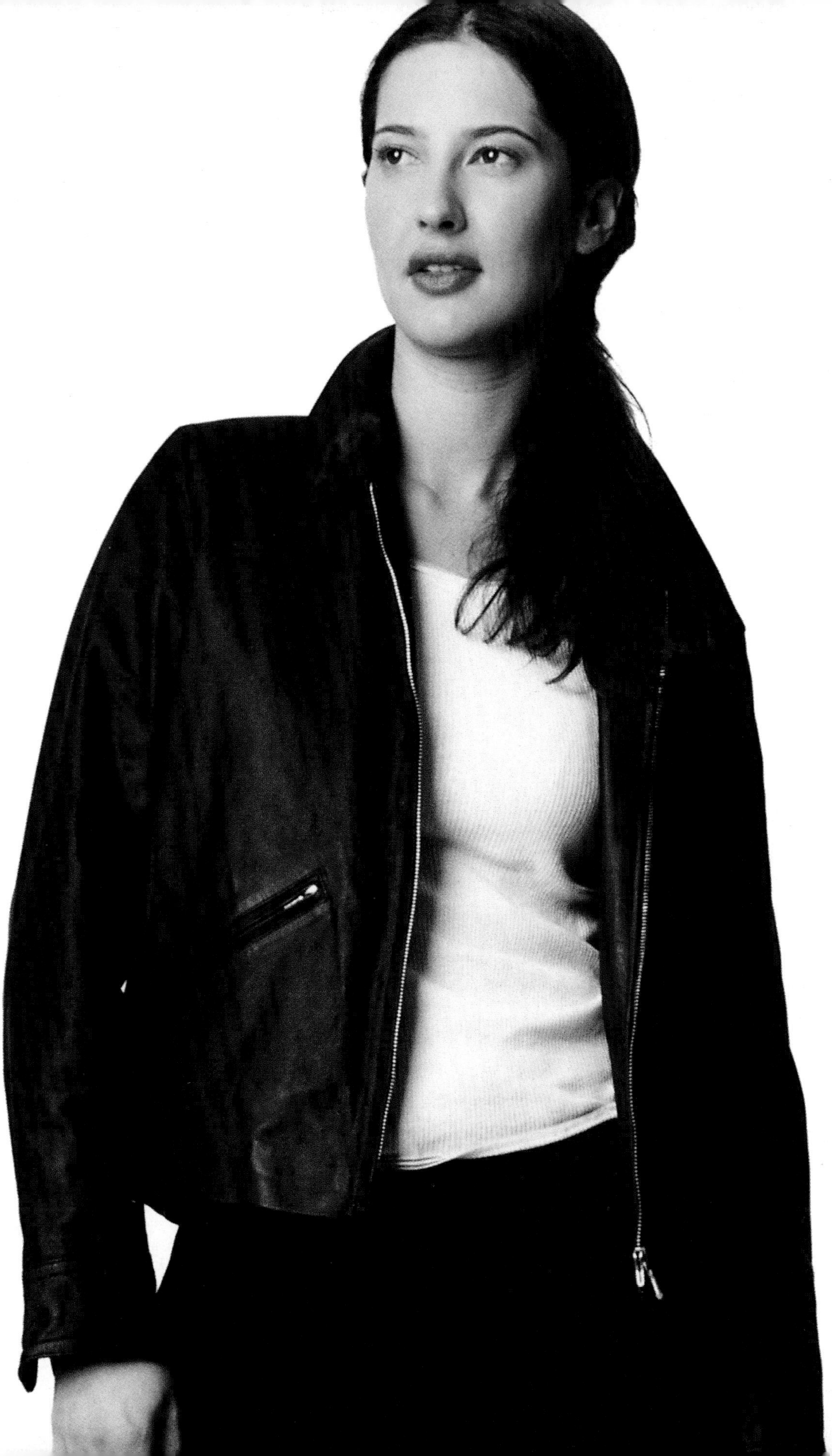

The Little Black Dress

We know one when we see one. It might be a chemise from the '20s or a sheath from the '60s, but it's always simple, elegant, slyly sexy, and unmistakably black. It's perfect for almost any occasion and it always makes us look good. It's magic, and it's been going on for more than eighty years.

Most people believe that Gabrielle Chanel invented the little black dress, but for once the great innovator was a little late. The genre dates back to the First World War, when simplicity, and black—the color of mourning—appealed to all. Many French designers made little black dresses during the late teens, although they were not recognized as such. It was Chanel who came up with that perfectly descriptive phrase, she who famously said: "Scheherazade is easy. A little black dress is difficult." In May of 1926 her "little black dress" appeared in *Vogue* and what had been merely simple became chic. Prohibition (1920–1933) also gave the genre a serious boost. Since bootleg liquor was only palatable in a cocktail, women were soon shedding their tea gowns in favor of cocktail dresses. Through the fabric restrictions of the wartime '40s and the wasp-waisted '50s little black dress endured, reaching something of an apogee in the 1961 film *Breakfast at Tiffany's*. In it Audrey Hepburn wore the same knockout, sleeveless Givenchy shift to cocktails at "21" and on a visit to Sing Sing, looking perfectly dressed at both. After a short hiatus in the '60s and '70s (when everybody was focused on pants), the little black dress returned to us in the sleeveless satin sheaths, slip dresses, and other simple, sexy styles of recent decades.

In 1997 it even inspired its own book, *The Little Black Dress*, in which author Amy Holman Edelman enlists the help of experts to analyze the genre's enduring appeal: Etiquette specialist Letitia Baldrige thinks that "because the little black dress is not conspicuous in shape or fabric, it imparts a certain mystery, inviting a man to draw physically closer to see its hidden details." Fashion publicist Eleanor Lambert says it's "for women with more to think about than their wardrobes," while fashion designer Mary Quant believes that "black can be all things to all women." But perhaps actor Walter Matthau said it best in his *Sex Tips for Girls*: "You'll never get laid looking like that," he told one young woman. "What you need is a simple black dress."

You need the right little black dress for you. You have many decades from which to choose. While almost every little black dress is inherently slimming, look for a silhouette that flatters your particular body type, then look for great tailoring, subtle detail, and beautiful fabric.

Versatile
VintageFinds

Here are a handful of perennials—patterns, materials, categories—that provide the best bang for your vintage buck. Think of them as "red flags" while shopping. If you see a beautifully beaded bodice or a print designed by Pucci, for example, take a closer look. You'll also find that there's always room in your closet for something great in leather, denim, silk jersey, tartan, or an animal print. And nobody can ever have too much beautiful, versatile vintage lingerie.

Denim

It's not just jeans—we're talking jackets, skirts, shorts, and shirts too. Denim is more of a way of life than a fabric and it's been that way for a long time. It saw America through the Depression, and by the end, as the uniform of the "workingman," it seemed almost to stand for America itself. It also evoked images of the cowboy, who by the '30s, egged on by Hollywood, had become another American icon. Thirty years later denim had shifted ground: It was now the uniform of rebellion, of "flower power" and free sex, "the secret signal among the freedom fighters in the American streets," as David Little wrote in *Vintage Denim*. This was a revolution everybody wanted to join

(or at least be perceived as joining), and denim entered the mainstream, going upscale with "designer jeans" while the traditional "worker's" styles remained the all-American, never-out-of-fashion street look. Worn in any form, denim conveyed a subtle, insistent message of youth, sexuality, confidence, and belonging. It still does.

Vintage denim is a big category. There are the standard Levi's and Lee jeans, skirts, and jackets made anytime in the '50 through '70s, the personalized, embroidered numbers made in the '60s, and the sleek designer jeans of the '70s, not to mention denim suits, dresses, overalls, jumpers, shorts, coats, and accessories. Some people collect the rare, historical examples, but that's another story. When you are buying to wear, look for denim classics that suit your figure and your lifestyle. Soft, broken-in, much-washed jackets in the familiar waist-length style are great on almost everyone. So are simple fly-front skirts with jean styling and, of course, jeans. They all cling in the right way, will never go out of style, and you can wear them with almost anything. Denim with nonjeans styling (the buttons, rivets, and distinctive stitching) can look slightly dowdy, so watch out. Do you really want a baggy denim jumper? Go for the magic.

Animal Prints

Until the '60s, the bold, graphic patterns of giraffe, leopard, pony, and zebra used by fashion designers were the real thing—the skin or fur of the animal—which made beautiful jackets, accessories, or decorative trim for suits and dresses. These were inherently luxurious materials. Everybody knew they were hard to come by and therefore expensive and desirable. When killing animals for their skins became politically incorrect (even illegal), designers were undismayed: They didn't need the animal, only the look.

It's a look that has never gone away. The patterns provided by nature as camouflage are so appealing, so beautifully designed that we can't get enough. There are other reasons too: "Our brains are hardwired to perceive certain animals as threatening," says Valerie Steele, chief curator at Manhattan's Fashion Institute of Technology. "We want to take that power onto ourselves by wearing their skins. It's like a trophy of the hunt. There are also a lot of positive cultural associations at work here. Cats are seen as sexy, snakes as dangerous, zebras as exotic." Because the perception of the pattern as "fur or skin" is also hardwired into our brains, a giraffe or leopard pattern printed on cotton is still perceived as luxurious and desirable.

No wonder designers have used these patterns in every decade for the past forty years. Think of Rudi Gernreich's famous 1966 head-to-toe giraffe print outfit, or Jean-Louis Scherrer's leopard print evening dress of 1977. There's an unending supply out there in the vintage world and almost any animal print garment, of any age, can be a winner. Flag anything you see and then examine it closely. Remember, you want only good-quality clothes that suit you. One other tip: Animal prints are best used in moderation. Don't mix them or overdo it, or you won't look sexy and rich, just tacky.

Jersey

Actress and courtesan Lillie Langtry—called "The Jersey Lily" after her island home—was celebrated in the 1880s for her stretchy, skintight dresses and the voluptuous figure they revealed. That combination, in the days when a glimpse of stocking was still looked on as something shocking, did much to popularize the fabric that soon came to be known as "jersey." It even inspired a popular song that began: "She wore a jersey fitting like an eel skin. . . ."

Jersey does cling, but it also drapes beautifully and therein lies the secret of the clothes of Madame Alix Grès, the couturière who made jersey famous. The young Alix had wanted to become a sculptor but ended up sewing for a fashion house instead. In 1934, when she was still in her twenties, she opened her own house and began to create draped jersey dresses that seemed to come straight from the golden age of Greece. She "sculpted" them right on the model, cutting and pinning until the pleats and drapes fell just right. Not surprisingly, they were a huge success. Over the decades Madame Alix Grès formalized and repeated a number of these patterns so that it became difficult to tell if a dress was made in 1944 or 1964. Each one is a masterpiece and would be a fabulous vintage find.

But you don't have to happen upon a Madame Grès to enjoy wearing jersey. Many designers have followed in her footsteps: In the '70s Vicky Tiel successfully emulated her style in jersey dresses, while Stephen Burrows did his own riff on the idea—edging his jersey creations with a lettucelike ruffling that emphasizes their smoothness, weight, and hang. Halston also used jersey to perfection, as has Giorgio di Sant'Angelo. Good-quality jersey by anybody is worth looking out for. The fabric's ability to drape and mold the figure is unparalleled. The right dress will look as if it was made for you. Nothing drapes or pleats so well or takes color so beautifully. Look for good-quality, pure silk jersey that's heavy and smooth, and a garment that suits your figure. A slim column of jersey is always beautiful, but pleating or draping can be very flattering. And don't stop at dresses: A jersey halter or wide draped jersey pants can be great finds.

Lingerie

This category is made up of garments that were originally made for bedroom and undercover wear but are now versatile choices for the street and everywhere else too. We're talking about slips, chemises, teddies, nightgowns, and peignoirs from the '20s to the '50s—made of silk, cotton, linen, and satin, in velvety black, silvery gray or colors like melting ice cream—handsewn, embroidered, or trimmed with lace. Even the rayon from the '40s and '50s feels and looks better than almost anything out there now. The world has changed a lot since these lovely things were made. Women no longer hide their assets under modest clothes and several layers of underwear. Fashion is all about showing off a trim, fit figure and what better way to do it than in garments that were made to do that in the first place (albeit in private). And talk about associations: Vintage lingerie drips sexiness. It's all about boudoir intimacies and undressing and revelations. It's also about glamour, about Rita Hayworth and Jean Harlow slinking around in peignoirs, and Elizabeth Taylor in that tight slip in *Cat on a Hot Tin Roof*.

All of this has not been lost on designers. Slip dresses, bustiers, corsets, camisoles, and peignoir style coats have long been a part of many of their repertoires. But unless these examples are couture or otherwise wildly pricey, they are likely to be less well made and of lower-quality fabric than the vintage lingerie from which they were copied. Why buy a cheap contemporary slip dress when you can buy a pure silk slip from the '40s for less? A '30s bias-cut nightgown makes a great evening dress. Silk lounging pajamas and marabou-trimmed bed jackets go out to restaurants and parties. A lace-trimmed teddy looks great peeking out from a tweed suit jacket. These are easy, inexpensive finds—so common that you can afford to be choosy, so hold out for the best colors, fabrics, and fit and make sure the condition is perfect. Wear bare, clinging things if your figure is up to it. Otherwise, go for the lounging pajamas and under-suit teddies.

Beading

Beading as we know it began in the early Victorian era when, in 1845, the "Glass Tax" was repealed and glass items of all kinds—beads among them—became much cheaper. These glass beads could be sewn onto clothes in a way that followed and accentuated a pattern, adding sparkle and a luxurious feeling. By the '20s, when beaded chemise dresses came to fashion prominence, the Victorian era was long gone and a little discreet sparkle wasn't enough. What women wanted were dresses that shimmied and shone, responding to their every movement.

Beaded fabric clings like no other, moves like no other, and because it catches the light, it draws attention to these other properties. No wonder Josephine Baker liked to knock 'em dead in shimmering beads. So did Ginger Rogers and all of the other Hollywood ladies who danced their way to stardom. Their beaded gowns moved so beautifully as they leaned back in the arms of Fred Astaire and Gene Kelly, catching the light as they pirouetted, making the wearers seem like rare, shining stars. In a way, they were. By the '40s the intensive labor required to sew thousands of tiny beads onto a dress by hand had become blindingly expensive. This only added to the allure of beaded creations—an allure that has continued until the present.

When in the '60s Balenciaga and Saint Laurent did beaded evening dresses or when Norman Norell and Bill Blass used beads to such good effect in the '70s and '80s, the very presence of these sparkly accoutrements underlined the fact that these were hand-made luxury clothes.

Beaded items from the '20s on are wonderful vintage choices. Nothing adds such luxury and sparkle to your wardrobe, for a fraction of the price you would have to pay for a contemporary example. You want good-quality fabrics and hand-sewn beads, but you certainly don't have to stick to pricey couture items. Look for shawls, evening sweaters, bolero jackets, and beaded dresses of all kinds. Make sure you like the style of the garment itself, that it suits you, and, above all, that it is in good condition. Beading by its very nature is fragile. Examine it carefully and then treat it gently when you get it home.

Tartan

The origins of plaid are lost in the sands of history—literally. The Egyptians were already wearing it in the first few millennia B.C. The word itself was coined in Scotland in the Middle Ages to describe the shawls of the poor. "Plaid" means "blanket" in Gaelic. Our associations with these colorful patterns, however, are much more recent, dating back only to the 18th century, when Scottish plaids or "tartans" (the term for the design and color) were first used to differentiate one clan from the other. It's a romantic idea—all of those brave Scotsmen proud in their plaid kilts and knee socks—roaming the lochs and glens of the Highlands. Queen Victoria certainly thought so. She loved tartan, and during the early part of her reign, new ones were brought out every fall. The new aniline dyes of the 1850s made the colors brighter and clearer, adding to her enthusiasm. Since then British royalty has always had a soft spot for tartans and when, in the 1920s, the charismatic Edward VIII (later the Duke of Windsor) resurrected his father's old tartan coats and such, he made them newly fashionable.

Designers were quick to pick up on these associations and the others that tartans were soon engendering. Their frequent use for school uniforms and "little girl dresses," for example, added a patina of innocence. Tartans seemed inherently pure and anti-fashion. What could be more irresistible for high-fashion clothes? Molyneux and John Fredericks showed tartan jackets, skirts, and blouses in the '30s. There were tartan utility dresses made during World War II and tartans by Balenciaga in the early '50s. All-American plaids were celebrated by Claire McCardell and Bonnie Cashin in the '40s, '50s and '60s. Designers from Giorgio di Sant'Angelo to Saint Laurent showed tartans in the '60s and beyond. Even Giorgio Armani has not been immune.

All of those associations can work for you. Go all-American with a red plaid shirt, or Lolita-like in a short tartan jumper. Have you always had a soft spot for Prince Charles? What's wrong with a long, swirling green plaid taffeta skirt? If you're not going to Balmoral this season, pair it with a slinky black top and some very, very high-heeled shoes. There is no end to the vintage tartan choices awaiting you out there. Just buy a good-quality example of something that looks good on you. You can wear it forever.

Do-it-yourself

Susan's '30s black lace nightgown cost $30 on amazon.com. Tiring of its full-length silhouette, she simply reaches for the scissors and creates a whole new look. The swath of lace she has removed from the hem would make a great shawl, but Susan has another idea. She uses it as a form-flattering cummerbund, changing the line of the dress. By letting her hem dip lower in back, Susan creates an asymmetrical handkerchief effect that is both hip and retro.

193.

How and Where to Shop for Vintage Clothes

Shopping for vintage classics is almost as much fun as wearing them. What could be more fun than choosing among hundreds of one-of-a-kind, beautifully made garments that flatter your figure and are easy on your pocketbook? Vintage is definitely a new, more rewarding way to shop—but you won't be joining the hordes at the local mall. Instead, you'll find yourself browsing interesting new venues from flea markets to on-line auctions. Shopping strategies will be different too. Because nothing you'll see is made today, there's no "backroom" stock in every size—every garment is the only one of its kind and each is different from the next. Vintage shoppers quickly learn to scan the varied bounty of many fashion decades and zero in on the styles and shapes that are right for them. It's a whole new world, but we know all the right moves. In this chapter we gladly share them with you.

Finding Your Personal Style

Find the body type you resemble most and you'll know which clothes will best suit your figure.

Let's face it: Nobody looks good in everything. Some clothes make us look "hippy" or "busty" or focus all eyes on our less-than-svelte middle region. Others seem to be magic—smoothing us out, skimming over our trouble spots, presenting us at our best. Those are the clothes we search for, season after season, sighing with frustration if designers don't provide them.

Stop sighing and shop vintage. One of the great advantages of this kind of shopping is the opportunity to choose among a host of flattering, classic silhouettes that may not be "in fashion" at the moment but always are in style. If the big shoulders, slim skirts, or hip-hugging trousers of the moment look terrible on you, why invest in a short-lived, unsuccessful look? Instead, go vintage and experiment with classic shapes from other decades. Try on circle skirts from the '50s, long skinny knits from the '70s, narrow sheath dresses from the '60s, or wide pleated trousers from the '40s. Stand back each time and check out the effect in the mirror. Do you look thinner, fatter, taller, curvier, or less curvy? Do you like what you see? If so, note the general shape of the garment and the decade in which it was made and add it to your mental "shopping list."

To help choose the shapes that might be right for you, think back to the "ideal" figures of recent fashion eras. Remember the pinup girls of the '40s and '50s? They were curvy— "full-figured"—as the saying goes, and they had tiny waists. Twiggy and the super-slender, androgynous look ruled in the '60s, while the statuesque, long-legged Jerry Hall carried the long, swirling, peasant looks and sleek Halston knits of the '70s and '80s with aplomb. Find the type you resemble most and you'll know what kind of clothes are likely to best suit your particular figure.

"I have a small waist," says Lauren, an avid vintage shopper, "so I tend to go for the fitted bodices from the '40s and '50s. On the other hand, I've found that bias-cut dresses from the '30s are really hard for me to wear. I never even try them on anymore." "I'm rather short, and I have curves," says Marianna, another experienced vintage buyer. "I also go for the '40s and '50s clothes. They fit me really well—much better than the straight-up-and-down 'mod' clothes from the '60s. I don't even pick those up anymore because I know they just aren't going to be flattering." Getting to this point of selectivity is where all vintage shoppers want to be: When you know what you are looking for, you can scan those racks with confidence, knowing that your hand will reach out toward the shapes and silhouettes that really work for you.

Where to Begin

So many fashion decades to explore. So many choices. What a fledgling shopper needs is a place where she can see and touch hundreds of vintage garments, all carefully organized and neatly displayed—where all the gathering has been done for her and she can browse and try on to her heart's content. An impossible dream? Check out your local specialty vintage boutique. These shops offer large selections of clothes in perfect condition, carefully chosen for their intrinsic quality and interest. They employ informed salespeople who love to chat and share their knowledge and offer clean, private dressing rooms (perfect for prolonged try-on sessions). As such, they are the perfect place to develop your "look" and your nose for classic style and fit. The only downside: The prices are considerably higher than those at the local thrift store. The owner has done the legwork for you—he has hit every flea market and yard sale to gather his stock and is now charging for his time, expertise, taste, presentation, and convenient location. You too will soon be nosing around these other venues—but if you hit the specialty stores first, you'll go with a trained eye that will save you time and money.

Browsing one shop may not be enough. Big-city girls in particular should visit a number of vintage shops to make sure they are seeing a true cross section of the market. In metropolises like New York City, Los Angeles and London, there are now so many vintage stores (over 1670 in NYC at last count) that some have begun to specialize quite narrowly—in denim for example, designer names, or '50s clothes. Most of these store owners have distinct personal styles that greatly influence the selection of their stock. One may be heavily into "swing" clothes from the '40s, another obsessed with Little Black Dresses or fascinated by '60s Mod London. Be sure to check out enough of these shops to find out what sparks your imagination and flatters your figure. You don't live in a large city? No problem. Almost every town now has at least one vintage shop and it is likely to carry a little of everything. To find your local vendor, consult the telephone directory, cruise the Internet, or ask any local antique dealer. They always know.

Shopping in a Specialty Vintage Boutique

Although it's not necessary to buy anything on your first few trips to a vintage specialty boutique—in fact, it is not recommended—when you have your act together and feel ready to make some purchases, here are some strategies to keep in mind.

When you enter a store that is new to you, do a quick walk-around to get the lay of the land. You're looking to see what decades the shop covers, whether the owner's taste is similar to your own, whether you are looking at racks of pricey designer names or more affordable material. It also helps to develop a mental picture of how the store is organized. Most shops divide their stock by sex (many also carry men's clothes—which can look great on women, by the way) and then by type of garment—trousers, dresses, skirts, etc. Some stores then organize these smaller sections by color; others group all the knits together, or all the clothes with designer labels. Some also set up specialty areas like "Swing Dresses" or "Black Dresses" or "Prom Dresses" for easy reference. Vintage clothes are never organized by size, however, and they are only rarely organized by decade.

Next, walk through again, picking up anything that looks promising. Because everything is one-of-a-kind, you'll want to grab it when you see it and either carry it around (to compare with other possibilities) or have it put in a fitting room or behind the counter until you can try it on. You can always put it back, but if you leave it on the rack, it may be gone on your next pass—nestled in the shopping bag of that smug, attractive blonde just leaving the store. At this hunting-and-gathering stage, keep an open mind. Although you may have come in with something specific in mind ("I really need a slim, black skirt"), look at everything with the same keen eye, and if you see a great beaded sweater that looks like it was made for you and goes perfectly with your favorite suede pants, don't hesitate. Be aware, however, that if beaded sweaters are very hot at that particular fashion moment, you are going to have to pay more for yours. Vintage store owners know exactly what's happening in current fashion and mark up their swing dresses or Jackie O sheaths when those shapes appear on the runway. No matter how much you pay, you'll probably end up with a better-made garment for less than you'd pay for the newest version.

While you are shopping, don't be afraid to chat up the store owner. Most vintage shop owners are on-site a good deal of the time, they love to talk, they are passionate about their subject, and many are extremely knowledgeable. You can learn a lot in the course of these friendly conversations. In Christina Bartolomeo's 1998 novel *Cupid & Diana*, for example, a vintage store owner called Mary takes the personal approach and starts the heroine on her way to savvy vintage shopping. "Mary never lied to me about what looked good and what didn't," writes Bartolomeo. "She never sold a customer an unflattering garment . . . From Mary I learned the designers who suited me and those who didn't . . . Mary loved the hidden beauties of good workmanship . . . a hem properly finished with lace basting tape, a lovingly worked buttonhole, a satin lining striped in old gold and rose. Fine craftsmanship brought joy to her heart." Become a regular at your local vintage boutique and find your own Mary. A friendly vintage store owner may help you streamline try-on sessions ("Don't bother trying that on, it's tinier than it looks" or "That would be fabulous on you"), offer to bring things out of the back to show you, or call you when something special comes in.

If you don't see anything you want on a given visit to your favorite vintage store, be sure to check back frequently. Remember that there are no seasons in vintage shopping—owners are constantly on the prowl for new stock and the stuff on the racks changes frequently. Meanwhile, spread your net widely. If you travel for business or pleasure, make this kind of shopping a part of your routine: Get out the telephone directory or go on the Internet and find the vintage shops in the towns and cities you plan to visit—the farther flung the better. The more distance you put between you and large urban centers, the lower the prices.

No matter where you shop, those prices are likely to be firm. Vintage shop owners consider themselves retail merchants, in the same league with Bloomingdale's or Harrod's, where it would not be appropriate to haggle. There are some exceptions: If you buy a number of things at once you might ask for a volume discount, and once you have established yourself as a serious buyer who is likely to be back next week and the week after that, you may find the owner will make accommodations here and there. Never, ever ask for a discount the minute you walk in, ask only when you're serious about buying a particular item, and be friendly and polite when you make your request.

Shopping at a Vintage Clothing Fair

In New York it's the "Metropolitan" and the "Pier Show"; in Santa Monica and San Francisco it's the "Vintage Fashion Expo"—regularly scheduled extravaganzas attracting vintage clothing dealers from all over the country. Each dealer rents a small booth or stall and fills it with his or her best merchandise, often saved for months for the occasion. The result: a gigantic vintage bazaar, with rows of minishops, often stretching as far as the eye can see. It's your chance to sample the best stock from the best dealers, coast to coast. These are major vintage happenings and worth the trip if your own town doesn't host such an event. While individual vintage shops may be the best place to identify which shapes and styles work best for you, fairs are the next best step in any vintage education. They provide the chance to see hundreds of examples of those shapes and styles—all under one roof. A fair gives you a shorthand, firsthand look at everything that's out there. Suppose, for example, that you are attracted by '30s bias-cut slip dresses. Before you buy one you need to know if such dresses are common or rare, the price range within which they usually sell, and the colors, materials, and ornamentation you are likely to encounter in the marketplace. Only then can you judge the quality and desirability of any given dress. At a fair you will see fifty such dresses and you'll soon know a good one when you see it.

Fairs are also one of the best bets for shoppers interested in older, pre-'60s clothes and for rare material of all kinds. In fact, anyone with a special interest—Victorian whites, '20s beaded dresses, '40s walking suits—will have a field day at one of these events. There are so many dealers that no matter what you are looking for, you can find a number who specialize in your decade or type of clothing. You can go right to the '50s dealers, for example, or to the dealer who does nothing but '70s leather, without having to wade through a lot of general interest stock. Such a fair is so big, in fact, that it is one of the only places that you can go with a very specific agenda—a Diane Von Furstenberg wrap dress in a particular hard-to-find pattern—and actually find it. If an item remains elusive, you can also network among these specialists, spreading the word about what you are looking for. They will call or E-mail you when they find it.

Size is the fair's chief advantage, but those endless rows of booths can make the whole experience a bit overwhelming. The best approach is to get organized: Do a preliminary, swift walk-around, checking out everything and jotting a few notes. You'll want to note the location of those dealers who carry the kind of thing you like or whose taste seems to match yours, and the numbers of the booths offering any likely garments you notice on your first pass. If you skip this walk-about, it's very easy to get stuck at the first dealer you come to. You could end up spending all your time and money there and then see something much better and cheaper a few booths up the aisle. If you are dying to stop and try something on, beg the dealer to put it on hold for half an hour. He or she may comply, especially if it's later in the day and they aren't being deluged with customers.

Once your walk-through is over and you are circling back to look carefully at specific pieces, the strategy changes: If you see something truly terrific and the dealer will not hold it, get ready to make a quick decision. There's a lot of competition out there and, if you hesitate, that Halston ultrasuede safari jacket you've been eyeing may disappear before you can say "Studio 54." Although it's always best to try things on, at big events that can be a bit of a problem. Some dealers will let you take clothing to the communal women's bathroom to try it on there (if you leave your driver's license, to make sure you are not tempted to grab the merchandise and run), or you can just slip things on under or over your clothes (more advice about that later).

Pricewise, fairs are at the expensive end of this market—about the same as specialty vintage stores. After all, these are the same dealers who run those stores back home, and when bunched together at a fair, small-town dealers tend to check out the prices of their big-city counterparts and raise them accordingly. As always, prices for currently fashionable shapes and styles will be much higher. (You can do best by shopping against the fashion grain, as long as what you buy suits your particular figure.) On the other hand, haggling is more acceptable. Dealers who have schlepped cumbersome station wagons full of stuff to the fair are anxious to sell it and not bring it home again. The closer to the end of the fair, the more flexible they are likely to be. Their pressure to sell is counteracted by the pressure on you to buy—now—knowing that the dealer is about to go back to Kentucky, say, and take that fabulous '50s pale blue pleated satin evening dress with her. With both parties so motivated, there's usually a way to work it out.

Shopping Flea Markets, Estate Sales,Yard/Garage Jumble Sales

To some vintage shoppers, going to specialty boutiques and fairs is like shooting fish in a barrel—there's no sport, no challenge, no chance to bag the big one. These are the girls who like to tell about the Versace cashmere sweater they picked up at the yard sale in the Hamptons for $5 and the entire box of fab '60s clothes they snagged at a San Antonio estate cleanout for $22. While prices at these venues can be ridiculously low and opportunities for steals abound, this kind of shopping is considerably more work and is best attempted by those who enjoy the process and know what they are looking for and what it is worth. After a couple of educational sessions at a vintage boutique or fair you too will be one of those lucky people and the fun can begin. There is no telling what you can find or how little you can pay.

It helps if you are an early riser. Flea markets get going as early as 6:00 A.M. and vintage store owners from near and far will be swooping down on the best stuff long before any sane person has had her coffee. So go as early as possible, or go just before closing time when disappointed dealers are anxious to unload anything not yet sold. Wear comfortable clothing (preferably something that will make trying on in public a bit easier), and carry cash, but only small bills—you don't want to flash a wad while you are bargaining—and a shopping bag. As you would do at a fair, do a quick walk-around and take notes. Then visit the likeliest stalls and examine the clothes that catch your eye. When you see something really good, try it on as best you can with no fitting room available, and if it fits, buy it on the spot. It's probably not very expensive and it won't be there when you come around again. Don't expect everything to be in perfect condition, or even very clean. Wear gloves if you want to, check carefully for damages and irreparable staining (more about that later), and forget about the rest. After one trip to a good dry cleaner your garment will be as clean as anything else you own.

Check out the booths of any vintage clothing dealers, of course, but at a flea market the best bets are often the general antique dealers who buy up households and are offering their contents. To these people, clothing is just so much bulk—to be sold by the pound—of much less interest than the silver, rugs, and porcelain they got in the same haul. They know little about it and they almost never take the time to find out. "Usually they've just bought everything in a house somewhere—including the closets," says one avid flea market hound. "The clothing may be on a rack, but often most of it is in boxes under the table. If you see any clothes, ask if there are more—here or even back at the dealer's house. The dealer may want you to buy a whole box but it's usually so cheap that if it looks promising, you won't mind taking the chance. Who knows? There might be a Chanel jacket at the bottom."

Estate and garage sales offer even more opportunity because the garments are still on the original premises and no dealer is involved. The dealers will be there, however, trying to buy, so you need to show up early. These affairs usually begin at a slightly more civilized hour—around 8:00 A.M. Be there when they open the door, wearing your comfortable "trying-on" clothes and carrying your gloves, small bills, and a shopping bag. If it's an estate sale, head for the bedroom where the clothes of the lady of the house are often laid out. Here you could be face-to-face with the situation vintage shoppers dream about—the discovery of an entire wardrobe of a person whose taste is much like your own, and in your size. Keep dreaming, and make her a rich person who shopped in Paris, whose heirs care more about her Sisleys than her Schiaparellis. It can happen. Such sales in resort areas like Palm Beach, Long Island, or Santa Barbara offer particularly rich possibilities, but don't worry if you are prospecting in suburban Kansas City or on the outskirts of St. Louis. Midwestern sales have yielded legendary vintage finds.

211.

At these temporary shopping venues bargaining is expected and you should never accept the first price you are quoted. Ten percent off is standard but you can sometimes do better. If you're a good actress, take out your pitiful stash of $1 bills and whisper, "I really love it, but I only have $30." Or take the practical approach: Buy a lot and ask for a volume discount; point out a stain, a tear, a drooping hem, or, if the garment is particularly small and so are you, remind the seller that very few other people are likely to be interested. As always, never ask for a better price unless you are seriously considering the purchase, and don't be rude or denigrate the material.

Thrift Shops

A thrift shop resembles a large, urban garage sale, although it is actually nothing of the kind. It is a shop run by a registered charity in which all merchandise has been donated and the proceeds go to benefit the cause. Donated merchandise can be anything from a used lawn mower to almost-new pots and pans and almost always includes plenty of clothing. Such stores differ tremendously depending on their location and the charity they serve. Good Will and Salvation Army stores often have more furniture and large items, while shops run by urban hospitals and other charities usually go for the small stuff and feature more clothing and accessories. Since most donors tend to come from the immediate neighborhood, the more affluent the locale, the snazzier the clothes on offer. Keep this in mind when vacationing in any resort area. Visit the local thrift in Palm Beach, East Hampton, Bar Harbor, Santa Barbara, or Harbor Springs and you'll find bits of the well-made—even couture—wardrobes of rich women packed in with the T-shirts and polyester dresses.

Resort areas aside, shops outside large urban areas usually yield the best hauls. Many thrifts in New York City, Los Angeles and London are now well aware of the value of vintage designer clothes and automatically skim these off before they reach the racks. They are then offered to local dealers, netting far more than the $3 or $10 charged for most thrift garments. But get out into small towns or, better yet, the country, where nobody's even thinking about vintage clothes and there, among the used washboards and tricycles in the corner, may be something you never thought you'd ever get a chance to buy. (New York City fashion designer Shannon McClean recommends the thrift shops of upstate New York, where she once found a fabulous '30s Schiaparelli fur coat for $50.)

To unearth a thrift shop treasure takes patience. "You have to be in the mood for this kind of shopping," says Stephanie, a veteran of New York's many thrifts. "You have to sort through massive quantities of junk. But it can be exciting." Persistence is more important than strategy, but there are a few recommended moves. If you know

213.

the day of the week when new merchandise is added to the racks of a particular shop, that's the day to visit. (Grace Logan of New York's Spence Chapin thrift store notes that her shop purposefully scatters these days so that dealers can't come in and pick off anything good immediately.)

Bring your own shopping bag and don't forget the gloves and the "trying-on" clothes. Approach with an open mind. There is no point in going to a thrift store with a specific objective. First check the store window where canny charity workers tend to put the most tempting outfits. When you attack the racks—which are usually organized by type of garment and are so closely packed that it is difficult to see anything properly—train your eye to look first for fine fabrics. In a sea of dusty, limp synthetics, the eye quickly learns to pick out the heathery, densely woven wool of a '40s jacket or the crisp cotton of a well-made '60s sheath. When you spot something of quality, quietly examine it further to determine if it is your size and style.

When you do spot something, don't wait. Grab it and put it over your arm for later consideration. There may be other vintage hunters (including dealers) just beyond you and as soon as you pull out a possibility, they will pounce. Remember, as you look, that this is a thrift store. Condition may not be optimum. Try to imagine the piece freshly dry-cleaned, with buttons replaced, re-pleating accomplished, or shoulder pads added. If it is cheap enough, you may want to take a chance on a garment that is slightly stained. You can always discard it if the stain doesn't come out. To get the best treatment from the management, become a regular at one or two stores you particularly like. You might just end up being the person called when something juicy appears. "You can get on somebody's list," says Grace Logan. "Come in, meet the manager, bring candy, schmooze." A couple of dos and don'ts: Don't try to negotiate—thrift shop prices are already low and you'll seem churlish since it's all for charity anyway. Do be careful of the "designer" clothes being offered at nonthrift prices. Unlike vintage shop owners, thrift managers don't always know what they are looking at and may mistake a designer's boutique or ready-to-wear line for the couture item and mark it up too high. If you don't know the difference, you could end up doing the impossible—overpaying at a thrift shop.

Consignment/ Resale Shops

People often talk about thrift and consignment shops in the same breath, but the two are quite different. While a thrift store funnels all of its proceeds to charity, a consignment shop is a plain old-fashioned business, selling gently used clothes on behalf of individual consignors and taking a profit on these transactions. There are other differences: Thrifts take whatever they are given while consignment shops are quite selective and accept only highly salable garments in perfect condition. You can find some interesting pieces in a consignment shop, usually those made sometime during the last ten years. Are they vintage? That depends on your definition. Technically anything no longer in the stores is vintage, and last season's pure wool, navy double-breasted Ralph Lauren blazer will look just as good on you this winter—and next. If no designer is showing a particular skirt shape you admired on the runway last year, this may be your best chance to get one without breaking the bank. Don't expect thrift store prices, however. That skirt might be priced at $150—an improvement on the $450 it cost new but still a chunk of change.

This is a good time to mention that other extremely reasonable and often-overlooked source of wearable vintage clothes—your own closet. Almost everybody has a few ten-year-old skirts, jackets, or dresses hanging limply in the back of an overstuffed closet—once-beloved items that seemed too good to give away. Chances are they are still perfectly wearable, and if you get them out, have them dry-cleaned, and begin to pair them up with items from your contemporary wardrobe, you'll find they work beautifully. If they were chosen originally with your figure type in mind, so much the better.

Don't forget to check the closets of your mother, grandmother, or Great-Aunt Louise. Any one of those ladies might have saved interesting things from her younger wardrobe and would be thrilled by your interest. Take old Mrs. MacDougal, whose closets inspire the heroine of Barbara Michael's novel *Shattered Silk* to change her life and become a dealer in vintage clothes. " 'There are a couple of Worths around somewhere. He made my trousseau. I was quite a clotheshorse in my day.' Mrs. Mac indicated a white net dress over-embroidered and banded with lace . . . 'And this.' She lifted a coat of gold and silver brocade whose collar and wide sleeves dripped sable." If you're thinking that such ancient finery is not for you, check with relations from more recent generations. They might just lead you right to a stash of '50s Chanel suits or Mary Quant Mod dresses.

Auctions

Auction houses are a rather specialized arena of vintage shopping. At these venues vintage clothes are treated as the rare, collectible objects they indeed can be. Sales are built around couture clothes, those associated with famous personalities like Marilyn Monroe or the Duchess of Windsor, or rare, quirky, or iconic examples geared to serious collectors and museums. Many of the bidders are not buying to wear but are bent on preservation and will carefully pack away their new acquisitions in acid-free tissue. Also, unless you live in New York or London you may have a hard time finding a vintage clothing auction to attend. At this writing, regularly scheduled sales are held only at William Doyle Gallery in New York. Christie's and Sotheby's offer clothes in their London salesrooms. Regional houses occasionally offer clothes as part of single-owner sales (the estate of a movie star or famous singer, for example), so check your local paper. Because the clothes are nearly always important or historical, prices are relatively high.

This doesn't mean that a canny, persistent person can never snag something beautiful, wearable, and reasonably priced at a vintage clothing auction. Most sales include a few such lots—like a nice full-skirted black chiffon by nobody in particular, ca. 1955, that slips by for $450 as other buyers concentrate on the Diors and Balenciagas. Auctions are unpredictable; it all depends on who shows up—or doesn't—and things sometimes do go cheap. If even the lower auction prices are beyond your price range, remember that the preview (a four- to five-day period when all of the clothes are on view and available for examination) is a wonderful opportunity to become familiar with the history of fashion and to see great examples from periods that interest you. At the very least, stop by the auction house and pick up a catalog. They are excellent educational tools, points of comparison, and sources of pricing information.

If you do plan to bid at a sale, always attend the preview and examine every piece carefully. Read the description in the catalog where any defects will be noted, along with the measurements of the garment, which will indicate how it will fit. If you want more information, ask the specialist in charge of the sale for a "condition report." To guide your bidding, the auction house provides an estimate, the range within which they expect a piece to sell. Often the lot will sell for far more and occasionally for somewhat less. You could leave low bids on a couple of pieces that the house will execute for you. That way you do not have to attend the sale and you will only buy if luck is with you that day and almost nobody else is bidding. You can also bid by telephone, if you set it up ahead of time.

Remember that any bid is subject to a 10 percent buyers' premium that is added to the price at which the auctioneer's hammer comes down. If you attend in person, try not to get carried away when the action starts. Establish a comfortable top price and stick to it. In fact, it might be a good idea to sit through a couple of sales to get a feeling for bidding rhythms and auction procedure before you ever raise that paddle (a numbered, plastic disk you raise to indicate a bid) and have a go at that tempting black cocktail dress.

Of course, not all auctions take place in New York or London. Country auctions are held constantly, all over the United States, in suburban or rural neighborhoods. At a country auction the protocol is much the same as in the city—there are a few days of preview, then the sale. There's usually a buyers' premium charged and you can arrange to leave a bid with the house. But there are also some differences: The material on offer will not be elegant or important examples culled from among many possibilities, but boxes of clothes that have come, along with living room furniture and pots and pans, from local estates. One lot may consist of several boxes so you might end up with a lot of stuff you can't use. But prices are often quite low, and if there's one wonderful piece stuffed into one of those boxes, you'll come out a big winner.

Just beware the killer tactics of some competitors: Back to Barbara Michaels's *Shattered Silk*, where our fledgling vintage dealer Karen gets a lesson in these nasty doings as she browses at a country auction. Her more experienced colleague explains: "' . . . she'll rearrange the boxes while you aren't looking . . . suppose you scrounge around in these boxes and find something . . . that one piece makes it worthwhile. So when your box comes up you bid,

219.

Photograph courtesy of Mary Hillard

and you get it cheap, and you think hip hip hurrah—until you take a closer look and discover the one item you wanted isn't there. By a strange coincidence it happened to work its way into the box Margie just bought.'"

It happens. So go to the preview and examine every lot carefully—and quietly. You don't want to alert other vintage browsers to a possible find—or tempt them to switch boxes on you. Since trying on is almost never an option, bring your tape measure and measure anything likely—country auctioneers don't provide that kind of detailed information—and don't forget that list of your own (honest) measurements.

ebaY

Browse | S

FA

It's about style — finding th

The Glitz

Vintage

<u>Clothing</u>
<u>Couture</u>

On-line Auctions and Web Sites

The worldwide web has created a brave new world of shopping possibilities and vintage clothing is no exception. You can now bid for vintage clothes on the many on-line auction services available, or browse the thousands of retail dealer web sites that make the clothes for sale in San Francisco or Bangor, Maine, as available as those at your neighborhood vintage store. UPS is all you need! The computer has effectively leveled the geographical playing field. The girl sitting at her screen in Bismarck, North Dakota, now has almost the same access to vintage material as the girl living at Second Avenue and 78th Street. The universe of available material on-line is virtually unlimited and it is also more organized than ever before—not to mention easier to use. You can ask the computer to show you only items with very specific silhouettes or only those by a particular designer; you can locate all of the vintage specialty stores in an area you are planning to visit and check their stock. It's an exciting new world of possibilities and it's growing bigger every day.

Computers are so magical that you can lose sight of their limitations: Remember that they cannot bring you face-to-face with the pieces under consideration. Unlike toaster ovens, baseball cards, and other generic items, vintage clothes are not standardized. Even after you've read the detailed description of a garment and seen the digitalized photographs the computer provides, you will not know how the garment will really look or how it will fit. You cannot touch the fabric, judge the wear, or try it on for size.

None of this will be a problem if you use the medium wisely. Before you start moving that mouse, take a few weeks to educate yourself about vintage clothes in the real-life off-line world of specialty shops, fairs, and flea markets. Look, touch, try on, immerse yourself in the subject. Learn what styles best suit you and the variety of clothes found in that style; learn which designers cut to fit your particular body, the usual prices of various items, and likely condition problems. Learn the right questions to ask. Armed with this information, you can then efficiently browse eBay.com, Sotheby's, Amazon.com and any other on-line auction sites that carry vintage clothes. Now, when you read the descriptions, study the photographs, and note the starting prices, you will know exactly what you are looking at and whether you want to bid. The same knowledge and experience helps when you're browsing retail web sites. Say, for example, that you have discovered that coats by '60s American designer Bonnie Cashin, size 8, always look great on you. You can punch in the keywords "Cashin" and "coat" and find every such coat available at retail, coast to coast, or through an on-line auction service. You can then contact those shops or bid through the auction service, and although you've never laid eyes on the coat in question, buy with complete confidence.

Come to your screen armed with your measurement information, ready to compare with the measurements provided by the dealer or auction service. While these numbers are of some help, unless you are sure about a designer's usual cut try to avoid garments that need to fit perfectly to look right. Skirts and pants are usually a better bet than jackets and dresses, with their more complicated tailoring. If you are unsure, ask for more information: If the item is being offered retail, E-mail or call the dealer to whom it belongs. Ask the dealer for more photos, a more specific condition report. Or, since on-line auctions last several days, E-mail the consignor (the person selling the item) and ask for the same kind of information. If you are shopping eBay, check the feedback letters on the person offering your lot, to find out if he usually describes his merchandise fairly and ships promptly. Learn the art of bidding at an on-line sale: You'll find that most people wait until the last few minutes of a sale to bid, then bid quickly again and again, until the last second. If you can't be on-line in those last moments of the lot's availability, some services will execute your bid automatically, up to the level you indicate. Once again, try not to get carried away. Have fun but remember that on-line bidding is so easy and anonymous that it can easily become an addiction. And how many beige Bonnie Cashin car coats can you really use?

Assessing What You See

Whether you are browsing on-line, strolling the aisles of a flea market, or visiting your local specialty boutique, you'll want to ask yourself these four important questions.

1 Is the style of this garment flattering to my figure?

2 Is this garment the right size?

3 Are its fabric and workmanship fine enough to make it a worthy addition to my wardrobe?

4 Is it in good condition?

If the answer to any one of these is no, you might want to think again before you buy.

Size

Size labeling is such an integral part of department store shopping that you may be surprised to find that vintage store tags don't provide this useful information. That's because vintage sizing is either unreliable or nonexistent. Standard sizing (the 2-14 scale that we are all used to) is a relatively new development, instituted during World War II. Before then blouses were sized one way (with numbers like 32A, much like a bra) and dresses another and both tended to change from decade to decade. Sizing was also less of a priority because so many pre-1960 clothes were made by little dressmakers and local couturiers for private clients. When clothes are made to measure, size becomes irrelevant. Postwar, off-the-rack clothes were officially sized but unless they were made after 1970, this information will leave you no wiser. Most posted sizes will be much smaller than you'd expect. A '50s size 8 is more like today's size 4 and size 14 is more like today's size 8. This has occasionally led to vintage shopper freak-out—so it's good to know up front that these numbers are meaningless.

Ignore them and take matters into your own hands: "I hold up a dress and pull it across my waist and bust to make sure the fabric goes around," says one experienced vintage shopper. Another has discovered that when it comes to trousers, just pull the waistband around your neck. If it touches, the trousers will probably fit. (Sounds crazy, but it's true.) If you're looking at a blouse or jacket, measure the garment's shoulder line against your back. Better yet, leave nothing to chance. Take your measurements before you leave the house. Be honest! Write down this information and carry it and a tape measure with you whenever you shop. That way you can compare your measurements with those of the clothes you like and you'll know immediately if something is worth trying on.

It's best to try on a prospective purchase. Many vintage clothes look awful on the hanger but because of their expert cut or draping, put them on the right figure and you've suddenly got something marvelous. "I remember one little black dress I got for $18," says Liz, a savvy vintage shopper. "It looked like nothing on the hanger and nobody was trying it on. I took a chance and wow!" Even when you're a whiz at recognizing the right dress or jacket for your body type, because every garment is a little bit different, you really need to see it on. If you get tired of running to the dressing room, dress creatively for your shopping excursions and try on right in front of the rack. Wear a bodysuit or tights and a camisole—anything sleek and tight—and pull things on right over your clothes, or wear a wide skirt under which you can pull something up. Once you've amassed a handful of things that will probably fit, repair to a dressing room, strip down to your underwear, and make your final decisions. And about that underwear: Many of these clothes were made for women who wore a whole layer of foundation garments under their clothes. "Wear a proper, structured bra when trying on structured clothes," warns a '50s aficionada. "Otherwise, nothing will fit. And if you are going for anything slinky or bias cut, you might even want to wear a girdle or at least something smoothing."

By this time you may well be wondering whether you should buy something that almost fits and have it altered. The answer is: sometimes. Shortening a hem won't change the way the garment hangs, but opening up seams to make something bigger or cinching in a too-large dress with a belt or adding shoulder pads may change it forever and dampen its appeal. Particularly if the garment is expensive, proceed cautiously. "You must have a really good alterations person for this kind of work," says author and vintage clothes aficionada Barbara Milo Ohrbach. "Find somebody who really knows draping and design and can work with something old." Of course, if you've spent practically nothing on a garment, or love the fabric but hate the style, rework to your heart's content. You may well come out with something more interesting and flattering than the original, which also fits you perfectly.

Quality

It may seem an odd point to make in a book extolling the joys of vintage clothes, but the fact that a garment is old does not automatically make it better. Old is just old. What you are looking for are vintage clothes of great quality and interest. One of the primary reasons for shopping vintage is the chance to buy a garment as beautifully styled and made as the couture clothes of today for less than you would pay for the cheesy, cookie-cutter stuff at the mall. This is easier to accomplish than you might think. Many pre-'60s clothes were made by hand, using beautiful fabrics that are now too expensive for most manufacturers to use—or that have ceased to be made at all. Look for great styling, expensive or intricate fabrics, interesting finishing touches, and first-class hand workmanship. These are the qualities that make a vintage garment a wearable classic.

Fabric

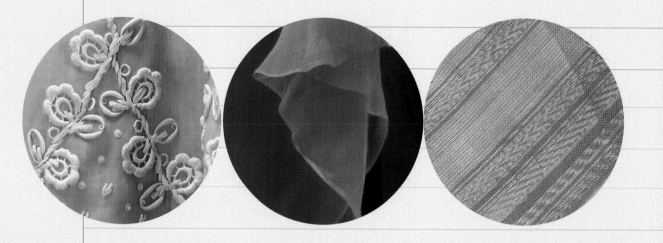

Vintage clothes should be appealing to the touch as well as your gaze. Run your hands gently along the fabric of an attractive garment. Is it an unusually satisfyingly heavy wool or a particularly filmy chiffon? Is the color brilliant or the pattern unusual? Many older fabrics were made by processes that are too time-consuming or costly for contemporary production. "They used much finer fabrics for the ordinary, nondesigner clothes of the '50s and '60s," says fashion designer Shannon McClean, a dedicated vintage shopper. Such fabrics may be particularly tightly woven, heavily embroidered, or have a more beautiful sheen than any available today. "You can find clothes in wool/silk blends that would be considered a couture fabric today," says McClean. "There's a heavy silk ottoman you'll see used that isn't even made anymore." Even the rayons made from the '30s to the '50s are worth looking out for. They are not synthetics (they were made from a tree fiber called cellulose) and bear little relation to the flimsy discount store stuff of today; they drape and take color beautifully. Color is another reason to shop vintage: "You'll see all kinds of shades you just don't see anymore—pistachio greens, turquoises, tangerines," McClean notes. "Women used to wear more vibrant color than they do now." Vintage cashmere sweaters, for example, come in unusual colors, and they are much thicker than the modern stuff to boot. You'll see impossibly soft, four-ply examples for less than the price of an ordinary Shetland.

Workmanship

A vintage garment is a veritable road map of clues to its origin, age, and quality. All you have to do is learn how to read the map. Start with labels—those little announcements of the maker and (sometimes) the city in which the garment was made. If there is no label at the back of the neck of a dress (or the waistband of a skirt or pair of trousers), don't give up. Feel along all of the seams of the garment. Particularly in couture clothes, you may find a label far down a side seam of a dress, skirt, coat, or jacket. Its absence, on the other hand, does not automatically mean the garment is not a couture item. Many labels proclaiming "Dior" or "Schiaparelli" were removed by canny travelers prior to going through customs.. That way, the duty owed by the well-dressed smuggler would be far less. If you see sheared-off vestiges of a label on an attractive garment, you may be on to something.

When a label is present, it can impart vast amounts of information. Does it say something like "Madame Dubois, Woodward Avenue, Detroit, Michigan"? The garment was probably created by one of the many little dressmakers working during the first six decades of the 20th century and will probably be extremely well made. Even labels from department stores can signal a good-quality find. Such stores often had their own couture departments. If the name on the label is totally unfamiliar it may still provide valuable clues: If it's woven (as opposed to printed) and sewn down on all four sides (instead of tacked at the corners), you can expect the garment to be of better quality. A union label, on the other hand, means that the garment was mass-produced.

Next, look at the construction of the garment. Turn it inside out and check for quality details like hand-set-in linings in interesting, contrasting colors or unusual materials. Check for interlinings made of more than one material (chosen for their use inside the garment) and generous seam allowances. Hand-stitching is not hard to spot. It is finer and more even than any machine can produce. A hand-stitched lining will look almost as beautiful as the outside of the garment. Overlocked seams that sew the seam and bind the raw edges with a continuous, machine-generated thread, on the other hand, usually indicate a more cheaply made piece. Is there a tailor's tack present? This is a series of x's in a contrasting color of thread, sewn at the front of a skirt or pair of trousers to indicate the front; it is found only in well-made clothes. The same is true for dress weights—small metal weights inserted to hold the line of a garment—hidden pockets, and lingerie straps (to keep bra and slip straps out of sight or to aid in hanging the garment).

Outside, you are looking for beautiful tailoring and for telling details like a pattern that has been matched so carefully that it continues smoothly from jacket to skirt. Be on the lookout for handmade buttonholes or those bound with strips of matching fabric, handpicked lapels, covered buttons, or interesting examples in horn, brass, pearl, jet, or bone. The presence of handwork like embroidery, appliqué or beading is always a plus. In general, you are looking for any unusual detail and/or workmanship no longer produced outside couture. Before you run to the cash register, however, check to see if the garment has been altered. Some alterations will change the way a garment hangs—and not for the better. Your eyes are the best tool for most of this quality-assessment work—but don't rule out touch. Take that '60s shift dress off the rack and heft it in your hand. Fine wool crepe, a hand-sewn, pure silk lining, and finishing touches like dress weights add up to a particular kind of garment that will feel good and look great on you.

PIERRE BALMAIN
COURREGES
PARIS
PAUL POIRET
a Paris
GRÈS
PARIS
Jeanne Lanvin
PARIS
UNIS FRANCE
15
Schiaparelli
21, place vendôme Paris
COURREGES
PARIS
PARIS

Condition

There are a lot of vintage clothes out there and unless you are considering a rare masterpiece like a Vionnet bias-cut number, you should not settle for anything in less-than-perfect—or near-perfect—condition. If an item is in the almost-perfect category, make sure the problem is something you can fix. Buttons can be replaced, and a tear along a seam can easily be resewn. A slightly unfresh odor will disappear at the dry cleaner. Other signs of age and wear will be with you always and should be avoided like the plague. If a shop is at all dark, take the garment out into the light to examine it properly. You don't want any surprises when you get it home.

Perspiration stains are the number one bugaboo in vintage clothes. Not only are they nauseous reminders of the garment's previous owner, they are absolutely permanent. Particularly if the garment is silk or linen, check carefully in the three major trouble spots—under the arms, at the waistline, around the neck—to make sure there is no staining. Mildew is another unfixable no-no. Run the other way. Ditto for rust stains on whites or stains that appear blurry and gray. They indicate an earlier unsuccessful stain-removal attempt and it is unlikely you will have any better luck. Wool garments stain less, but moths can be a problem. Always check for moth holes because reweaving is very expensive and even if a hole is small, it may cause the garment to begin to unravel.

Other irreversible signs of wear include shininess (which occurs when a fabric is past its prime), discoloration, fading, sagging, and drooping. No amount of cleaning or blocking will fix the problem. Carefully check the condition of any lace or beaded fabric. These tend to fall apart fastest. When looking at silk or cotton clothes made before 1950, make sure serious deterioration has not begun. Pull gently on the stitching along the seams. It should not pull away or start to disintegrate. In particular, check silk garments for the syndrome novelist Barbara Michaels immortalized in the title of her novel *Shattered Silk:* Around the turn of the century, fabric manufacturers used metallic salts in a finishing substance that added weight to the silk. Unfortunately it caused rot to set in—but just along the warp. The garment eventually tore into distinctive parallel strips known in the trade as "shattered silk.'"

Last Words

If, having read this chapter, you are tempted by the possibilities of vintage clothes but are one of those stubborn souls still hung up on the idea that they once belonged to somebody else, consider this interesting fact: Whether you are shopping at Neiman Marcus, Barney's, or Selfridge's, fifty other women probably tried on that black sheath before you came along. Some of them probably wore it out to dinner with the tags still on and then returned it to the store. Don't let misplaced squeamishness get in your way.

Instead, get out there and have fun. You'll love the clothes and maybe the competition as well. Remember, there's only one of everything. To keep your edge, practice self-control: Never grab something off the rack and crow "How fabulous!" Examine the garment casually, without calling attention to yourself. That way, every other shopper in the store won't rush over to try and snag your find, and if you plan to bargain, you won't have tipped your hand. Conversely, if somebody else has been too obvious and is loudly considering something you might want yourself, showing interest will only hasten her decision to buy. Keep away and hope she'll decide against it. Lastly, to avoid having to practice these Machiavellian tactics on your own best buddies (what a nasty thought), never go shopping with anyone who wears the same size or likes the same look as you do. There are few things as important as a great vintage find, but friendship is one of them.

List of Selected Vintage Dealers

There are vintage dealers in almost every city and town across the United States and Europe. A complete list would be impossible to compile, but the following dealers represent a good starting point for your explorations. Each one offers good-quality, wearable vintage clothing of the kind described in *Vintage Style*. Most operate retail shops; others are by appointment only or should be contacted through the web. Happy hunting.

New England

Karen Augusta
31 Gage Street
Westminster, Vermont 05101
(802) 463-3333

Artifice
307 Main Street
East Greenwich, Rhode Island 02818
(401) 734-9920
By appointment

Dragonfly
1297 Cambridge Road
Cambridge, Massachusetts 02139
(617) 492-4792

The Closet Upstairs
223 Newberry Street
Boston, Massachusetts 02116
(617) 267-5757

Dressing Up
154 Briar Brae Road
Stamford, Connecticut 06903
(213) 322-5285

Joel Weber
30 Broad Street
Milford, Connecticut 06460
(203) 877-6050

New York State

Brenda Jackson
50 Ripley Place
Buffalo, New York 14213
(716) 882-8732
By appointment

Right to the Moon Alice
240 Cooks Falls Road
Cooks Falls, New York 12776
(607) 498-5750

La Vie en Rose
7376 South Broadway
Red Hook, New York 12571
(914) 758-4211

Mark Walsh
78 Wendover Road
Yonkers, New York 10705
(914) 963-1694

Resurrection
217 Mott Street
New York, New York 10022
(212) 625-1374

Ina
101 Thompson Street
New York, New York 10012
(212) 941-4757

Cherry
185 Orchard Street
New York, New York 10002
(212) 358-7131

Patricia Pastor
19 East 71st Street
New York, New York 10021
(212) 734-4573
By appointment

Screaming Mimi
382 Lafayette Street
New York, New York 10003
(212) 677-6464

Mid-Atlantic States

Nonchalance
616 South Third Street
Philadelphia, Pennsylvania 19147
(215) 238-0525

Polyester Place
3797 Main Street
Manayunk, Pennsylvania 19127
(215) 482-4499

The Cat's Pajamas
335 Maynard Street
Williamsport, Pennsylvania 17701
(570) 322-5580

Revival Vintage
186 Center Avenue
Westwood, New Jersey 07675
(201) 722-9005

The Midwest

Rage of the Age
332 North Butler Boulevard
Lansing, Michigan 48915
(517) 482-2560
By appointment

It's In the Past
5436 Oldgate Drive
West Chester, Ohio 45069
(513) 777-5423
Mail order only

Blue Mirror
2531 Ticonderoga
Schereville, Indiana 46394
(219) 365-3825
contact by website:
bluemiro@jorsm.com

AdVintageous
101 Glenlake Avenue
Park Ridge, Illinois 60068
(847) 823-8451
By appointment

Just Faboo
107 East Main Street
P.O. Box 3913
Midway, Kentucky 40347
(606) 846-5606

The South

Evelina
799 Allendale Road
Key Biscayne, Florida 33140
(305) 365-9482
By appointment

Reminiscing Vintage Fashions
1579 Monroe Drive
Box 200
Atlanta, Georgia 30324
(404) 815-1999
Sales by mail only

The West

Lily
9044 Burton Way
Beverly Hills, California 90211
(310) 724-5757

Decades
8214 Melrose Avenue
Los Angeles, California 90046
(323) 655-0223

The Way We Wore
1094 Revere Way No. A29
San Francisco, California 94124
(415) 822-1800
By appointment

Wasteland
7428 Melrose Avenue
Los Angeles, California 90046
(323) 653-3028

Vintage Kats
807 West 12th Street
Austin, Texas 78704
(512) 457-0655

Five and Dime Vintage
606 East 13th Street
Denver, Colorado 80203
(303) 861-4979

Adair Appraisals
1311 Devon Glen Drive
Houston, Texas 77077-3211
(713) 861-7731
By appointment only

Flashback
50 Essex Road, Islington, London N1.
0207 354 9656

Pop Boutique
6 Monmouth Street, London WC2.
0207 497 5262

Retro
34 Pembridge Road, Notting Hill, London W11.
0207 792 1715

What's New Pussycat? The Hayloft, Stables Market
Camden, London NW1
0207 255 3036

Annie's Vintage Costume & Textile
10 Camden Passage,
Islington, LondonN1
0207 359 0796

Cornucopia
12 Upper Tachbrook Street,
Pimlico SW1
0207 828 5752

Yesterday's Bread
29 Foubert's Place, London W1
0207 287 1929

Stitch Up
45 Parkway, Camden, London NW1
0207 482 4404

Toffler Pruskin Decorative Arts
Flat 8, 6 Colville Houses
London W11 1JB
0171 221 2306

Steinberg & Tolkien
193 The Kings Road, Chelsea
London SW3 5EB
0171 376 3660

Modern Age and Vintage Clothing
65 Chalk Farm Road
London NW1
0171 482 3787

Blackout II
51 Endell Street
Covent Garden, WC2
0171 240 5006

The Gallery of Antique Costume and Textiles
2 Church Street
London, NW8 8ED
0171 723 9981

The Antique Clothing Shop
282 Portobello Road
0181 964 4830
London W10

MARKETS

Greenwich Market
London SE10

Portobello Market
Portobello Road,
(Ladbroke Grove End),
London W10 and W11

Camden Market
Camden High Street,
London NW1

CHARITY/THRIFT SHOPS

Oxfam Originals
26 Ganton Street., London W1
02074377338

Salvation Army Charity Shop 9
9 Princes Street, London W1
02074953958

AUCTIONS

Christie's South Kensington
85 Brompton Road, London SW7.
02075817611

Sotheby's
34-35 New Bond Street, London W1
02072935000

WEB SITES

Beverley Birks
www.camrax.com/pages.birks

Meredith Vintage Collection
www.meredith.com.au/vintage

Trashy Diva
www.trashy-diva.net

Vintage Couture
www.vintagecouture.com

The Paper Bag Princess
www.paperbagp.com

The Wastleland
www.thewasteland.com

Enokiworld
http://www.enokiworld.com/handbags3.htm

Piece Unique
www.pieceunique.com

Decades
www.decades.com

Ebay
www.ebay.com

Sotheby's
www.sotheby.amazon.com

How to Care for Your Vintage Finds

Vintage clothes—or any other quality garments—look better and last longer when they receive proper treatment and cleaning. With a little time and effort, yours will see you through many decades to come.

General care tips

• Always do up all buttons, zippers, and other closings, so that your garment hangs properly and does not wear unevenly or loseits shape.
• Cover your wooden hangers with a stuffed batting covering. The softness will be easier on your clothes and they will not come into contact with the wood, which can eventually cause a damaging chemical reaction.
• Always remove dry-cleaning bags immediately; they smother your clothes. To protect against dust, cover your garments with cotton sheets.
• Dry-clean or wash clothes immediately when they are dirty—don't leave them sitting in a damp hamper. But don't clean them more than absolutely necessary.
• Find a dry cleaner with his own equipment on the premises and who is a member of a professional association. Such a cleaner must take direct responsibility for the job he does and he is also likely to be more experienced and knowledgeable.
• When dropping something off at a dry cleaner, point out any stains that might need to be pre-treated or receive extra attention. Check your garment as soon as you pick it up so that you can discuss any problems before you leave.
• Before using any stain remover, test it on a small, inconspicuous area, blotting with white, absorbent fabric to see if the color is (oops) coming off with the stain.
• After you have worn a garment, leave it out overnight so that air can circulate around it.
• Heavy wool garments should be brushed after wearing to remove dust. If loose dirt is left to settle in creases, it will hasten a garment's deterioration.

- You can vacuum your garment to remove surface dirt. To avoid seeing your garment sucked halfway up a dirty tube, place a nylon screen (or even a mesh colander) between the vacuum and the clothes, and use the vacuum's soft brush attachment.
- Mothballs may be put near woolen clothes to discourage nibbling—but not in direct contact with them. Over the long haul the chemicals in the mothballs may cause damage.
- If you are wondering whether to dry-clean or hand wash, here's a general guide: It's best to dry-clean any garment that has interfacings or linings or is made up of two or more fabrics. Dry-clean beaded garments or those containing metallic thread.

Specific Care Suggestions

Sweaters: To hand wash, use cool water and a gentle product like Woolite or baby shampoo. Do not wring or pull the sweater out of shape, although you may rub gently on dirty collars or cuffs. Rinse thoroughly until the water runs clear. Lay your clean sweaters on a glass or wooden surface covered with a clean white towel (a colored one may bleed). A commercial drying rack (easy to buy) will hasten the drying process considerably. Squeezing the cuffs and waistbands together may help keep their form. Sweaters may also be safely dry-cleaned.

To get rid of those annoying "pills" that inevitably build up, stretch the sweater flat and clip the little buggers with your nail scissors or one of the cutely named products sold for this purpose.

Never hang your sweaters (they will stretch out of shape), and do store those made of wool with mothballs when the summer comes.

Beaded or sequined garments: These garments should not be hung—they may tear under their own weight. Store them folded in acid-free tissue paper. They may be dry-cleaned—but not more often than necessary. If you decide to replace lost beads by yourself, back the area on which you are working with a piece of netting to help hold the beads in place. Old sequins are made of a gelatin substance, which may lose its color or even dissolve when washed. Consult your dry-cleaning professional.

Silk garments: These may be dry-cleaned or hand washed in cool water—with some caveats. Don't rub them or wring them out, or a chalky bloom, caused by broken fibers, may appear. Watch out for patterns—they can run. Spot cleaning may leave rings. Hang to dry on a coated plastic hanger or dry flat. All taffeta garments should be dry-cleaned. Older silks should not be hung or folded. They should be rolled. Chinese silks should be given to a cleaner who knows how to deal with old embroidery.

Cotton and linen: Overpressed linen can become unpleasantly shiny. Steam it in your shower and press it while still damp. Velvet should always be dry-cleaned, never hand washed or pressed. If you are caught in the rain in your velvet opera cape, get it to a dry cleaner before it spots. Corduroy and denim items may be put in the washing machine. Turning them inside out will help preserve them. To remove rust marks from white cottons or linens, stretch the stained fabric tight over a pan of boiling water and sprinkle lemon juice on top. Rinse well, repeat as necessary. Alternatively, spread the stain with cream of tartar, and hold it over a steaming kettle. Rinse immediately.

Stain removal tricks: Some of these are a bit chancy—even bizarre—and should not be used on anything valuable or rare.

Makeup: Rub stain with a slice of white bread.

Ring around the collar: Rub stain with shampoo.

Perspiration stains: Rub with a paste of baking soda or table salt and water.

Or: Sponge with a tablespoon of white vinegar in a cup of water.

Or: Apply a paste of cream of tartar, crushed aspirins and water. Leave on for 20 minutes, rinse well.

Ink: If fabric is washable, spray with hairspray.

Protein or blood stains: Try toothpaste—not gel—without colors or additives.

Grease: Plain water will cause a grease stain to set. Always add detergent.

For other spots: Try diluted ammonia and glycerin or diluted hydrogen peroxide, or check out the commercial brands with the funny names sold in notions stores—Zout, Whink, etc.

Lisa Anastos
Neva Anton
Kelli Ayres
Debbie Bancroft
Beverly Banker
Hamish Bowles
Samantha Boardman
Serena Boardman
Muriel Brandolini
Bobbi Brown
Susan Ciancialo
Amy Fine Collins
Milly de Cabrol
Carrie Elliott
Liz Goldwyn
Alexandra Golinkin
Pamela Gross
Bethann Hardison
Gale Hayman
Elizabeth Hayt
Lisa Heiden
Deborah Hughes
Ranya Idliby
Kalliope Karella
Hayley Keenan
Lalta Keswani
Alexia Landeau
Sloan Lindemann
Eva Lorenzotti
Maria Macaya
Ghislaine Maxwell
Shannon McClean
Marian McEvoy
Evyan Metzner
Su Lin Cheng Nichols
Shyama Patel
Holly Peterson
Andrea Pomerantz-Lustig
Emmanuelle Ritchie
Kathryn Ross
Marina Rust
Beth Shepherd
Brandin Smith
Lauren Sweder
Judy Taubman
Michelle Tolini
Madley Unda
Vanessa von Bismarck
Jennifer Vorbach
Alexandra Wentworth
Patricia Wexler
Stephanie Winston